THE iPAD® IN THE MUSIC STUDIO

To access online media visit:
www.halleonard.com/mylibrary

Enter Code
2026-1857-1874-9639

quick **PRO**
guides

THE iPad® IN THE MUSIC STUDIO

Connecting Your iPad® to Mics, Mixers, Instruments, Computers, and More!

Thomas Rudolph
and Vincent Leonard

Hal Leonard Books
An Imprint of Hal Leonard Corporation

Published in 2014 by Hal Leonard Books
An Imprint of Hal Leonard Corporation
7777 West Bluemound Road
Milwaukee, WI 53213

Trade Book Division Editorial Offices
33 Plymouth St., Montclair, NJ 07042

Printed in the United States of America

Book design by Adam Fulrath
Book composition by Kristina Rolander

Library of Congress Cataloging-in-Publication Data
Rudolph, Thomas E.
 The iPad in the music studio : connecting your iPad to mics, mixers, instruments, computers, and more! / Thomas Rudolph and Vincent Leonard.
     pages cm
 Includes index.
 ISBN 978-1-4803-4317-7
1. iPad (Computer) 2. Sound--Recording and reproducing--Digital techniques. I. Leonard, Vincent A. II. Title.
 ML74.4.I477R82 2014
 780.285'41675--dc23
                                        2014025829

www.halleonardbooks.com

To my mentor and friend, Dr. Gerald M. Hogan.
  —Thomas Rudolph

To the memory of Elizabeth McGuigon and Helen M. Nick.
  —Vincent Leonard

CONTENTS

Chapter 1

Chapter 2

Chapter 3

Chapter 4

Chapter 5

Chapter 6

Chapter 7

Chapter 8

Chapter 9

Acknowledgments

The authors, Tom Rudolph and Vince Leonard, would like to thank the following individuals for their help and assistance with this publication: John Cerullo, Brad Delava, David Fair, Paul Geissinger, Bill Gibson, Andre Houser, Al Joelson, Jack Klotz Jr., Carole Kriessman, Lauri Leonard, Brian Lowdermilk, Hillary Money, Steve Oppenheimer, Liia Rudolph, Christopher Sapienza, Jackie Serratore, and Dave Roberts. Special thanks to Bruce Bartlett for granting permission to use his microphone diagram graphics in chapter 5 on pages 86 through 95.

INTRODUCTION

The iPad in The Music Studio is the second of two iPad-related publications by the authors. The first book, entitled *Musical iPad*, focused on music apps and music education. This book, *The iPad in the Music Studio*, focuses on the iPad applications for professional, project, and home music studios, live DJ applications, and publishing and distributing your music. The book includes an overview of the iPad and essential concepts, including selecting and connecting MIDI keyboards, DJ-related apps and gear, multitrack software, connecting an electric guitar and bass, external microphones, audio interfaces and docks, and using the iPad with audio mixers and Mac and PC music software. *The iPad in the Music Studio* provides guidance on the best apps and gear for music production.

This book is designed for both novice and experienced iPad users. If you are a beginner iPad user, we suggest you start with chapter 1 and proceed sequentially through the text. Also, you may want to consider reading the first book of this series, *Musical iPad*, as this publication only focuses on iPad apps for music and music education.

Companion Website

The book is only part of the learning experience. Each chapter includes links to video demonstrations of apps and gear. Also, the website will keep current with new apps that come into the market. For those of you who purchased the print version of this book, the video tutorials have a QR code printed. These look like this:

Figure 1. Hal Leonard website
www.halleonardbooks.com/ebookmedia/119488

You can use your smartphone or iPad to read the codes and take you directly to the link. If you don't have an installed QR code reader, you can download one from iTunes.

Quick Scan—QR Code Reader by iHandy Inc. (Free)
https://itunes.apple.com/us/app/quick-scan-qr-code-reader/id483336864?mt=8

We welcome your feedback. Please feel free to contact us with your comments: Tom Rudolph (tom@tomrudolph.com) and Vince Leonard (vince@vinceleonard.com).

THE iPad® IN THE MUSIC STUDIO

Chapter 1
iPad Basics

This chapter is an introduction for readers unfamiliar with the basics of the iPad. If you already own an iPad and are familiar with its operation, general settings, memory management, and transferring and managing files, you can scan the contents of this chapter and move on to chapter 2.

The iPad Is Launched

When the iPad launched in August of 2010, it created a new type of mobile device: the tablet computer. This combined the portability of a smartphone with a screen size close to a small laptop. Though initially criticized as nothing more than a large iPod Touch, Apple's music- and game-oriented version of the iPhone, the larger screen provided software developers with more options than the limited screen size of a smartphone such as the iPhone. Since the iPad and the iPhone share the same brain, or operating system, the iPad can run the applications already created for the iPhone. With new apps designed specifically for the larger iPad screen, there quickly became so many apps that books like this are needed to get through all of the options.

Music Friendly

With the iPad continuing to be more and more popular, the software and hardware add-ons for music hobbyists, students, teachers, and musicians are growing at a rapid pace. The iPad has established itself not as a toy but as a serious production tool. For the music studio, it's an external controller for studio hardware and software, as well as a synthesizer or sampler. For the performing musician, it can be a tuner, metronome, music folder, and effects rack. For songwriters, it is a sketchpad and portable studio. On gigs, it can record the concert. But yes, you can also use it for many other purposes, such as playing games and checking your e-mail. The main focus of this book is on how the iPad can be used to enhance the music studio, either for a dedicated music recording/production studio or a home-based studio.

iPad Versions

Since its inception in 2010, the iPad has been produced in a variety of versions. As of this writing, there are five versions or generations of the iPad. These include the following:

- The original iPad launched in April of 2010. It has a screen size of 9.7 inches.
- The second-generation iPad 2 launched in March of 2011.
- The third-generation iPad was released on March 16th, 2012. Apple dropped the numbering system and just referred to it as the iPad. The media refers to this as the iPad 3.
- The fourth-generation iPad was introduced on October 23rd, 2012. The media refers to this as the iPad 4.
- A new, smaller version of the iPad was introduced in October 2012, called the iPad Mini. It has a 7.9-inch display, compared to the 9.7-inch display of the iPad models.
- The iPad Air was introduced in October of 2013, and featured a much lighter and slimmer design.

The various models of the iPad can be reviewed on the Apple website: www.apple.com/ipad/compare/. As of this writing, the options include:

- iPad Air: Most powerful option available, with a 9.7-inch display.
- iPad Mini: 7.9-inch display.
- iPad Mini with Retina Display: 7.9-inch display.

iPad Connectors: 30-Pin and Lightning

When you purchase your iPad, it comes with the appropriate cable, which is used to connect to your computer to transfer files and charge the unit. There are iPads with two types of connectors. A 30-pin connector was the standard in the early days of the iPad.

Figure 1.1. iPad 30-pin to USB connector cable that ships with the iPad 2.

All other iPads are equipped with the newer Lightning connector that is standard on all iPads sold today: http://store.apple.com/us/product/MD818ZM/A/lightning-to-usb-cable?fnode=3a.

Figure 1.2. iPad Lightning to USB connector
cable that comes with the iPad Air and iPad Mini.

Cable Adapters

An important consideration if you are planning to connect your iPad to studio gear
(see chapter 2) is that you want to be sure you have the proper connector. There are
adapters to convert from Lightning to 30-pin; however, be sure that any external gear
you plan to purchase will work with the connector on the iPad: http://store.apple.com
/us/product/MD823ZM/A/lightning-to-30-pin-adapter?fnode=3a.

Figure 1.3. Lightning to 30-pin adapter.

Wi-Fi and Cellular

The other choice you must make when purchasing your iPad is whether to go with a
Wi-Fi or Wi-Fi and cellular option: www.apple.com/ipad/compare/. The advantage of
the Wi-Fi and cellular is that you can access your mobile cellular service to connect
to the Internet. So you can connect anywhere there is a Wi-Fi or cellular signal. You
will pay more for the Wi-Fi and cellular option, and if so, it will be tied to your mobile
phone service. The cellular option is a convenience that can be helpful; for example, if
you are in a recording studio that does not have Wi-Fi, you can access the Internet via
cellular service.

Memory

Another important consideration is the built-in memory your iPad has. Unlike computers, the memory cannot be upgraded, so when purchasing, be sure to purchase the memory that suits your needs. In our book *Musical iPad*, memory was not that important of an issue, as the applications in that book are apps that run on the iPad. However, since some of the applications in this book require more iPad memory, getting the maximum possible is a consideration. As of this writing, the options for memory configurations include:

- 16 GB (gigabytes)
- 32 GB
- 64 GB
- 128 GB

The best advice is to purchase as much memory as you can afford, even if it appears to be more than you need at this time. And be sure to check the memory requirements of any applications you plan to use. These will be covered in the chapters that follow.

iPad Controls

iPad Air

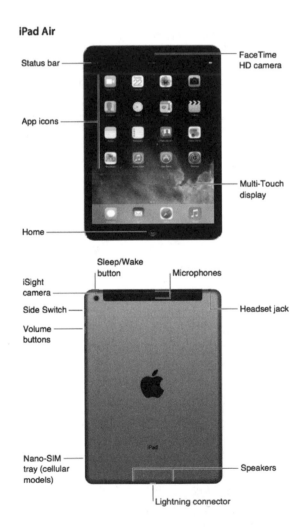

Figure 1.4. iPad Air Controls.

The iPad external controls include:

- A power button that also functions as a Sleep/Wake button.
- Two volume controls.
- A slide switch that can alternately mute audio or lock the orientation to portrait or landscape.
- A single Home button on the bottom, located in the center below the screen.
- Other options (see Figure 1.4)

All iPads since the iPad 2 have two cameras: one on the upper-left corner of the back and another that is centered in the border above the screen. There are two ports: a stereo mini headphone jack on the top left and a port on the bottom. The iPad is powered by a rechargeable battery, and it can be charged by plugging its docking cable into a computer's USB port or into its power adapter.

To operate the iPad, all you need is your finger. Press the Power button on top of the screen, and the iPad comes to life. For those familiar with the iPhone, the iPad works in a similar manner, only it is larger. The iPad experience is all about the larger screen size. When smartphones were launched, it was cool to watch TV shows or movies on a phone, but on the iPad, you now can actually see the details on the screen. The same can be said for computer game interfaces; more room allows for more attention to detail. The iPad is easily portable, and anyone can learn to use it in minutes.

iOS

The operating system for the iPad—the software it uses to perform its basic functions—is called iOS. The "i" was first used by Apple when it introduced the iMac in 1998, and back then it stood for Internet. Now Apple uses the "i" with many of their products: iPhone, iPod, iTunes, iBooks, and software suites iWork and iLife. The letters "OS" stand for operating system. So iOS is the Apple operating system that is used on Apple's mobile devices, including the iPhone and iPad. Apple continues to update the iOS, and every time they do, they add a number to it, such as iOS5, iOS6, iOS7, and so forth. It is usually a good idea to install the latest version of the operating system.

Once the iPad is activated, the Home screen appears, with a background photo and neatly arranged icons. Each icon represents an "app," or application, that is installed on the iPad. The icon positions are fixed by the operating system in five rows of four in portrait orientation, or four rows of five in landscape.

Figure 1.5. iPad in Landscape mode.

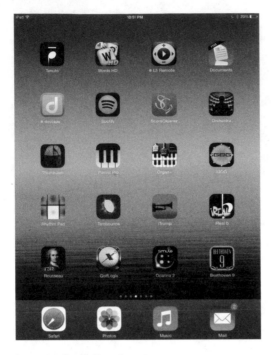

Figure 1.6. iPad in Portrait mode.

iPad Settings

There are some important iPad settings to be aware of when using the device with music gear.

Auto-Lock

To access the iPad settings, tap Settings. In the General Settings pane, tap Auto-Lock. Here you can set the amount of time that elapses before the iPad automatically locks or turns off the display. The choices are "Never," "15 minutes before," "10 minutes," "5 minutes," or "2 minutes." This is an important option, especially when you are recording audio or video or using the iPad to control other music applications where time is a factor. Some music apps have their own auto-lock settings, so check to see if you need to address this in the app settings or via the iOS settings described here.

> **Tip:** The Auto-Lock feature does not affect other options—for example, making adjustments to the volume or receiving notifications such as e-mail.

Airplane Mode

Airplane mode (http://support.apple.com/kb/HT1355) turns off the iPad's built-in wireless connections, including Wi-Fi, cellular, and Bluetooth—whichever is included in your version of the iPad. When in Airplane mode, you can't access the Internet or use anything that requires access to the Web, such as e-mail.

Airplane mode is an excellent option when recording audio or video or using your iPad with other music apps, since it won't be interrupted by any incoming messages or notifications. Another advantage is that the iPad's battery will last longer in Airplane mode. When you are in Airplane mode, a small Airplane icon appears on the status bar in the upper left-hand corner of the screen.

Battery Life

The battery life of the iPad is a consideration when you are using it for prolonged periods of time. Airplane mode has the added benefit of saving battery life. Some additional ways to maximize battery life include the following (www.apple.com /batteries/ipad.html):

- Be sure to use the latest iOS software. Often, newer versions will optimize battery use. Go to Settings and tap Software Update.
- Managing the screen brightness can extend iPad battery life. Auto-Brightness adjusts iPad screen brightness based on ambient lighting conditions, therefore minimizing battery drain. Adjust your brightness when indoors in a non-bright environment by going to Settings > Wallpapers & Brightness and dragging the slider to the left to dim. After making this change, turn Auto-Brightness off and then on again to reset to the default option.
- Turn off any apps that are running in the background.
- Lock your iPad when you aren't using it. To lock your iPad, press the Sleep/Wake button. You can also set the Auto-Lock interval as described previously in this chapter.
- Turn off Push Mail, and fetch data manually. The more frequently e-mail or other data is pushed or fetched, the quicker your battery may drain. To turn off Push and fetch new data manually, go to Settings > Mail, Contacts, Calendars > Fetch New Data, and set Push to Off. Then set Fetch to Manually. Messages sent to your push e-mail accounts will now be received on your iPad based on the Fetch setting rather than as they arrive.
- Minimize use of location services. Applications that actively use location services, such as Maps, may reduce battery life. To monitor location usage, go to Settings > Privacy > Location Services. If you see an application that you do not expect to be consuming battery power, you can disable it by setting the switch next to the application to Off. To disable all location services, go to Settings > Privacy > Location Services, and set Location Services to Off.
- For proper reporting of the battery's state of charge, be sure to go through at least one charge cycle per month (charging the battery to 100 percent and then completely running it down).

Tip: Some of the music interfaces introduced in chapter 6 will charge the iPad while connected.

VIDEO 1.1. SAVING BATTERY LIFE ON THE IPAD.

Figure 1.7
http://youtu.be/J8b-u1dwlGk

What's an App?

I'm sure you've heard the phrase "There's an app for that." The word *app* is an abbreviation of "application," which refers to a program that runs on a computer or other device. I'm writing this text on a word processor application. These computer programs include applications such as Microsoft Word and Apple Pages. Applications usually refer to programs that run on a Mac or Windows computer. The term *app* or *mobile app* is used to describe programs that run on mobile devices such as the iPhone and other smartphones, and the iPad and tablet technologies produced by companies other than Apple.

The concept of an app was first introduced with the iPhone, Apple's smartphone. Software developers create applications for the iPhone using Apple's iOS. They then post the apps to Apple's "App Store," to be purchased by anyone with an iPhone. The instant popularity of the iPhone took the app industry along with it. Apps can be created by almost anyone, and the cost is minimal when compared to computer-based software for Macs and PCs.

Native App

With computers, if you have a Windows computer and you want to run Microsoft Word or any other program, you must purchase the version that is written to run on that computer's operating system. If you want to use Microsoft Word on a Mac, you have to purchase the Mac version. In other words, there are applications that are "native" to each computer's operating system.

The same is true with smartphones and other devices such as the iPad. Each of these devices has a unique operating system, or OS. Some operating systems include iOS (Apple devices), Android, BlackBerry, Windows Phone, WebOS, and others. The iOS operating system was developed by Apple and is used to run iPhones and iPads. Just as Microsoft makes two versions of their software for Mac and Windows, so do developers of mobile apps often create several versions that can run on multiple mobile devices made by different manufacturers.

App Store

An app store, or "applications marketplace," is usually created and maintained by a specific vendor, such as Apple, Google, Intuit, and others. As an iPad user, you will be purchasing your apps from the Apple App Store. The App Store sells apps for all Apple products, including Apple computers, iPhones, and iPads.

> **Tip:** Starting with Apple's Mountain Lion operating system, the App Store has been built into the Apple operating system. This makes purchasing and installing apps a snap, and you can purchase apps via your computer or iPad.

The App Store makes it easy to search for and read reviews of apps that you are considering adding to your device(s). When you search for apps in the App Store, you can read about the application, including reviews posted by other users.

Mobile apps are usually free or very inexpensive. The prices of apps, including those mentioned in the *Musical iPad*, are usually under $5. In this book, premium music apps can top out in the $49.95 range. Once you purchase an app, there are usually additional purchases that can be made. Thus, adding apps to your device won't break the bank when compared to computer-based music software.

You can view the App Store on a computer or on your iPad or iPhone. If you are on a computer, point your web browser to www.apple.com/osx/apps/app-store.html. On an iPhone or iPad, launch the App Store app.

Managing Document Files in iOS

There is one major difference with iOS devices such as the iPhone or iPad when compared to Mac and PC computers. Namely, with iOS devices, the files associated with an app are not visible, as they are on computers in document folders and the like. iOS keeps all related files hidden, accessible only by running the app.

For example, if you purchase a song on iTunes, it will only be visible and accessible after launching iTunes. Download a movie, and it will only be visible and accessible by first launching Videos. Even the text documents created by the app Pages, Apple's word processing program, are only revealed after launching the app.

Managing documents is handled in several ways. All of Apple's apps are cloud based, so a file created in Apple Pages is automatically synched with Apple's iCloud service. Once stored in Apple's iCloud service, it can be accessed by any computer or iOS device synched to your account. The document can be archived by saving it to a computer and storing it on a backup drive or writeable media. The cloud is described later in this chapter.

Transferring Files via iTunes

Documents can also be transferred to and from the iPad using iTunes. For this process, the device must be connected to your computer using the 30-pin or Lightning cable. Select your iPad as the device, select the Apps tab, and scroll down to File Sharing at the bottom of the Apps screen to manage all of the documents that can be transferred to and from the iPad. Only apps capable of creating and loading files will be listed here.

VIDEO 1.2. MANAGING FILES AND APPS WITH ITUNES.

Figure 1.8
http://youtu.be/jMirahyIdmo

The Cloud

Throughout the chapters that follow, there will be mention of cloud applications such as Dropbox, iCloud, Google Drive, and others. The cloud, or *cloud computing*, received its name from the use of a cloud-shaped symbol to help you understand the complex nature of the technology. Cloud computing uses remote services such as computer file servers, usually on the Internet, where a user can store data, software, and other files.

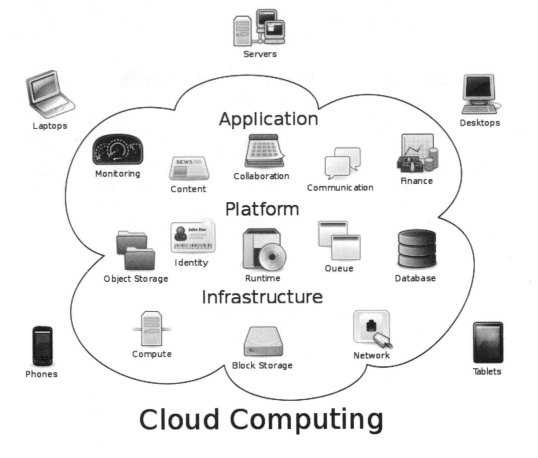

Figure 1.9. Cloud computing.

For musicians and for the sharing of the files in this book, services that allow for the posting and sharing of individual files are the best option. These include Dropbox, Google Drive, and Evernote, as well as others.

Cost: Free (Almost)

All of these services share a common format. They offer a limited amount of storage for free. When you exceed the initial storage capacity, you have a couple of options: delete files from your account, or sign up for a paid option that provides more storage space.

I use several services, including Google Drive, Dropbox, and SoundCloud. Each has its own advantages and disadvantages. However, for the purpose of storing files for music, which we will cover in the chapters that follow, a file-storage option is something that will save you time.

Dropbox

Dropbox users can transfer files to and from an iOS device and share these files with others.

Figure 1.10 Dropbox.

The main advantage of storing files in the cloud is that you can access them from your computer, smartphone, or iPad, as long as you have a connection to the Internet. You can post files from all of these devices, and you can share files with others. Before selecting your service, check to see what each offers. Some important questions to ask are:

- How much free storage is made available?
- How much will it cost for additional storage?
- How easy is it to share posted files with others and my other applications?

Your account is set up on one of these services and uses a password for access. Your information and data are as safe as with services such as Facebook, Twitter, and other online accounts.

VIDEO 1.3. DROPBOX.

Figure 1.11
http://youtu.be/BQT0bOoJ3as

Apple's iCloud

Just like Apple's mantra "Think different," their cloud service, called iCloud, is not the same as the services described earlier in this chapter. The difference with iCloud is that it works in the background and syncs files from your devices: iPad, iPhone, and computer. The operating system of the device actually does the synching for you: www.apple.com/icloud/. Unlike Dropbox or other services, there are no folders, and you can't drag a file to iCloud and then share it with others manually.

I use iCloud as a backup for certain aspects of the devices I use. It is indispensable when you set up a calendar, and then you can see any changes made on other devices. It works like this:

- Set up iCloud as the cloud service for some or all of the documents and shared items, such as calendars, on all of your devices.
- When you change something on a document or calendar, it is automatically sent to your iCloud account without you needing to do anything manually, as long as you are connected to the Internet.

Apple's iCloud does have a place to help you back up and share files. However, for storing specific files for use on your iPad and other devices, going with a service such as Dropbox or Google Drive is a better option.

Networking

The iPad is designed to be a wireless device. It can download e-mail and attached files, apps, music, video, and OS updates without being tethered to a computer or Internet router. Wireless communication is very powerful and versatile, but not without its share of potential problems. One tiny gap in communication from iPad to device may result in the link being lost, requiring a manual reset. The same may occur when an app stops working, referred to as a crash. This can be a liability, so it is good to have a backup plan ready to go at a moment's notice.

Memory Management

There are two things that fill up the available memory in your iPad: downloading apps and associating files with specific apps where the files reside directly in your iPad's memory. Since, as mentioned previously in this chapter, the memory of an iPad cannot be upgraded, purchasing an iPad with more memory than you think you initially will need is a good starting place.

Checking Memory Usage

Since the iPad is designed for ease of use, a lot of the behind-the-scenes information, including memory usage and file storage, is not readily available. The place to start is checking to see the status of your iPad's memory usage. Then, if needed, you can remove unused apps to free up space on your iPad.

VIDEO 1.4. IPAD MEMORY USAGE.

Figure 1.12
http://youtu.be/V7IliFxTyKo

Photos, Videos, and Music

You can choose to store photos, videos, and music on your iPad. However, since all of these files take up space, in order to maximize your storage, you can remove them from the iPad and either store them on your computer, where you can access them via iTunes or associate them with iCloud, or use other cloud-based storage, such as Dropbox.

Ask yourself if you need ready access to these files—for example, if you don't have access to Wi-Fi. If so, then leave them on your iPad. If you don't need them, store them remotely and access them when needed.

The easiest way to move these files from the iPad is to connect the iPad to your computer and, using iTunes, move the associated files to the computer (see Video 1.2) or to iCloud. Be careful when moving to iCloud, as you get a limited amount of free storage, and once you exceed this amount, you will need to sign up for one of Apple's paid iCloud accounts: http://support.apple.com/kb/ht4874.

iPad Accessories

Throughout this book, there will be references to devices that can enhance the music studio. Since the iPad is easily transportable, it is a good idea to invest in materials designed to protect it when you are using and transporting it.

Apple Accessories

There are accessories that Apple produces for the iPad. These include a cover, dock, and wireless keyboard. You can purchase these either when you order your iPad or after the purchase: www.apple.com/ipad/accessories/.

iPad Smart Cover

I highly recommend the iPad Smart Cover. It is excellent for protecting the iPad, and it can be used to adjust the viewing angle.

iPad Dock

An iPad docking station gives you a personal hub, which, when connected, gives you access to a port for syncing or charging and an audio line out port for connecting to powered speakers via an optional audio cable. These will be addressed in chapter 6.

Apple Wireless Keyboard

This typing keyboard uses Bluetooth technology, so it can be used with both computers and your iPad. This gives you a physical typing service for your iPad. If you do a lot of typing on the iPad, it is a valuable accessory to invest in.

Third-Party Accessories

Third party refers to companies that are not associated with the manufacturer but supply materials for the device. There are many companies that specialize in creating innovative products for the iPad, including cases, external keyboards, and more.

Cases

You've made a big investment in your iPad, so it makes sense to get a good case, just as you would for your other musical hardware and instruments. You can purchase a carrying case for the iPad such as those made by Otter Box (www.otterbox.com), Hard Candy Cases (www.hardcandycases.com), and Speck Products (www.speckproducts .com/tablet-ipad-cases.html). I use the Speck Handyshell, which has a handle that can be useful for many applications, including when playing a music app. Expect to pay $30 to $75 for a carrying case.

Figure 1.13 Speck Handyshell.

Cases with Typing Keyboards

Another option is to use a case and typing keyboard combination. As with other accessories, there are a host from which to choose. The Logitech Keyboard Case by ZAGG for the iPad includes a carrying case and a physical typing keyboard: www .zagg.com/keyboard-cases/index. Other options include the Kensington Keyfolio: www.kensington.com/kensington/us/us/s/1615/keyboard-foliocases.aspx.

If you do a lot of typing, this is something you will want to add. These combo cases and keyboards are priced in the $75 to $125 range.

Chapter 1 Activities

1. Check the iOS on your iPad. Do you have the latest version? If not, install it.
2. Rearrange the icons on your iPad, and create several folders to organize your iPad apps.
3. Connect your iPad to your computer and run iTunes. Review the process for copying files for specific apps.
4. Check the memory allocation on your iPad. Remove any unwanted apps to free space.
5. Open an account for cloud storage with a service such as Dropbox.
6. Create a wish list of accessories you want for your iPad. Put them in priority order.

Summary

This chapter reviewed the history of the iPad, the versions that Apple has introduced, and the two types of connectors used. The basic operation of the unit was addressed. The operating system, iOS, important settings, and memory allocation were described in detail. File management was reviewed with reference to using iTunes and cloud-based computing. Apps were defined and accessories explored to enhance the iPad experience.

Chapter 2
CONNECTING MIDI KEYBOARDS AND CHOOSING A STAND

This chapter addresses connecting a single MIDI keyboard to your iPad. For connecting multiple MIDI devices, refer to chapter 6. The advantage of using an external MIDI keyboard is that you have a physical piano keyboard for note entry in addition to using the iPad's screen. This chapter also reviews iPad stand options for the music studio.

> **Tip:** If you are unfamiliar with any of the music tech terms in this chapter or throughout this book, you can look them up online. One excellent option is Sweetwater's Glossary: www.sweetwater.com/insync/category/glossary/.

Choosing Your MIDI Instrument

Before considering ways to connect a MIDI keyboard to your iPad, choose the best MIDI keyboard or input device for your use. After you select the MIDI keyboard for input, then the proper MIDI adapter should be chosen. If you already have a MIDI device you want to connect to the iPad to use with music apps, then you are ready to select the MIDI interface.

MIDI Keyboard Types

There are two categories of MIDI keyboards: those that only connect via USB and those that connect via MIDI in and MIDI out ports from the instrument.

Step 1: Choose the MIDI Keyboard, Type of Keys, and Features

There are several considerations when selecting the best MIDI keyboard: features, size, and price. After choosing the best keyboard, select the appropriate connecting device, covered later in this chapter.

Keyboard Portability

If size and footprint of the keyboard is a main consideration, then consider purchasing a compact keyboard controller. This includes keyboards with mini- and full-size piano keys and other features.

> **Tip:** When purchasing gear, be sure to buy from an authorized reseller, as you will get the advantages of tech support and knowledgeable sales people. I do purchase items from places like Amazon.com and eBay.com; however, when it is a piece of gear that may require some tech support, purchasing from a music reseller is the best way to go. Companies such as www.sweetwater.com and www.musiciansfriend.com, as well as stores such as www.guitarcenter.com, offer discounts and support on music gear.

Mini-Size Keys

The smallest option is to go with a keyboard featuring mini-sized piano keys. The advantage is that these devices can fit in a coat pocket. The disadvantage is that the keys are smaller than normal piano keys or full-sized keys. The cheapest ones have very little more than just the piano keys. Other options include pitch bend and other knobs and controls on the keyboard.

iRig KEYS with Lightning ($129.99 list price)
www.ikmultimedia.com/products/irigkeys/

The iRig KEYS with Lightning connects directly to the iPad Lightning connector. It does not require any other connector or interface, as long as you are going direct to the iPad. It also includes a 30-pin plug, so it can attach directly to iPads with this plug configuration. The specs include 37 keys or three octaves, it takes up minimal space on your desktop, and it can easily fit in a backpack or carry-on bag. Features include:
- Modulation and pitch bend wheels.
- Volume/Data knob (assignable).
- Octave/Program Up/Down back-lit, soft-touch buttons.
- SET button to store and recall four different customized setups.
- Input for an optional sustain or expression pedal.
- Core MIDI (iOS) and USB class compliant (Mac/PC)—plug and play.

Figure 2.1. iRig KEYS with Lightning.

VIDEO 2.1. IRIG KEYS WITH LIGHTNING DEMO.

Figure 2.2
http://youtu.be/lbgx-aeJ0IM

Novation Launchkey Mini ($124.99 list price)

http://global.novationmusic.com/midi-controllers/launchkey

The Novation Launchkey Mini includes 25 synth-action keys for two octaves to play with at a time. In addition there are 16 tricolor pads to trigger loops, launch samples, and input drums or other instruments. Novation Launchkey and Launchpad apps are available for free from the Apple App Store. Compatible with iPad via the Camera Connection USB Kit (introduced later in this chapter).

Figure 2.3. Novation Launchkey Mini.

VIDEO 2.2. NOVATION LAUNCHKEY MINI DEMO.

Figure 2.4
http://youtu.be/0YCxhxWasl8

Tip: To view other options in the mini-sized keyboard area, go to your favorite music store or website and search for "iPad/iPhone Mini Keyboard Controllers."

Full-Sized Keyboards with 25 or 37 Keys

The next category is portable keyboards with full-sized keys. These options are usually 25-key or two-octave keyboards that include various other options.

Novation Launchkey 25 ($199 list price)

http://global.novationmusic.com/midi-controllers/launchkey

The Novation Launchkey series has an option similar to the Launchkey mini mentioned previously, except that the keyboard has 25 full-sized keys or two octaves. It requires the Apple Camera Connection Kit.

IK Multimedia iRig KEYS PRO ($149 list price)

www.ikmultimedia.com/products/irigkeyspro/

IK Multimedia has an option similar to the iRig KEYS with Lightning model mentioned previously. The difference is that the keyboard has 37 full-sized keys, or three octaves. It also comes with cables that connect directly to the iPad via either 30-pin or Lightning.

Line 6 Mobile Keys 25 ($149 list price)

http://line6.com/mobilekeys/

The Mobile Keys 25 gives you 25 velocity-sensitive, synth-action keys (two octaves) in a class compliant design that makes it compatible with virtually any music software or iOS app. There are even inputs for expression and sustain pedals for more control over your sound.

Figure 2.5. Line 6 Mobile Keys 25.

Tip: All of the iOS-compatible MIDI keyboards will also work with a Mac or Windows computer. However, there are some MIDI controller models that require power via USB, such as the Akai, M-Audio, and others not specifically designed for iOS use. You can use most of these keyboards with your iPad, but you will need to connect them from a powered USB hub. The powered USB hub supplies the power to the device. For example, a Korg Nano requires USB power that the iPad cannot supply. So connect the Nano to a USB-powered hub (http://en.wikipedia.org/wiki/USB_hub), and then connect the powered hub to the iPad via the Apple Camera Connection Kit adapter.

Full-Sized Keys: 49 or More

The next option is a keyboard that is not portable, so it won't fit in your briefcase, purse, or carry-on bag. These keyboards are designed for studio use, and they provide full-sized keys with four or more octaves, so they can more easily be played with two hands.

Novation LaunchKey 49 ($249 list price)
and Novation LaunchKey 61 ($299 list price)
http://global.novationmusic.com/midi-controllers/launchkey

Novation's Launchkey 49 and 61 USB/iOS MIDI controllers provide the ability to comfortably play two-handed parts. The keyboard has 49 synth-style keys, or four octaves, and the 61 has five octaves. Also included are nine faders and buttons, eight encoders, and dedicated transport controls. Sixteen velocity-sensitive, multicolor trigger pads let you play percussion, or start loops. Simply connect it to your iPad via the one of the options mentioned later in this chapter, and you are ready to enter via this instrument into music apps such as GarageBand, as well as Novation's free Launchkey and Launchpad iPad apps.

Figure 2.6. Novation Launchkey 49.

Line 6 Mobile Keys 49 ($199 list price)
http://line6.com/mobilekeys/

Connect it to your USB-equipped computer, your iPad, or your iPhone, and take control of your software instruments anytime, anywhere. The Mobile Keys 49 gives you 49 keys (four octaves) of velocity-sensitive, synth-action keys in a class compliant design that makes it compatible with virtually any music software or iOS app. There are inputs for expression and sustain pedals for even more control over your sound.

Figure 2.7. Line 6 Mobile Keys 49.

VIDEO 2.3 LINE 6 MOBILE KEYS 46.

Figure 2.8
http://youtu.be/GTLM2TfJUFk

Roland A-49 ($299 list price)
www.rolandus.com/products/details/1242

The Roland A-49 MIDI keyboard controller features a high-quality, velocity-sensitive synth-action keyboard in a trim, roadworthy package that weighs in at under six pounds. It offers USB and iPad compatibility, as well as onboard control of Roland SuperNATURAL-powered synths. Also included are assignable knobs and switches, octave and transpose buttons, sustain and expression pedal inputs, and Roland's bend/mod lever and D-BEAM controller.

Figure 2.9. Roland A-49.

Weighted 88-Key Keyboards

So far, all of the keyboards mentioned have synth- or organ-like keys. They do not "feel" like an acoustic piano. What manufacturers do to give the feel of playing an acoustic piano is add weight to the keys; hence the term *weighted keys*. This category also features keyboards with a full 88-key complement, the same as the standard acoustic piano.

Yamaha P-105 ($999 list price)
http://usa.yamaha.com/products/musical-instruments/keyboards/digitalpianos/p_series/p-105/?mode=model

Yamaha's P-105 digital piano with 88 weighted keys strives to emulate the sound and feel of a real acoustic grand piano. Built around the sound of Yamaha's CFIIIS concert grand piano, it emulates the dynamic feel of real acoustic piano strings. It connects directly to the iPad via the Apple Camera Kit USB connector.

Figure 2.10. Yamaha P-105.

Roland A-88 ($1149 list price)
www.rolandus.com/products/details/1243

The Roland A-88 MIDI keyboard controller gives you Roland's Ivory Feel-G Keyboard with Escapement in a trim, roadworthy package that offers USB and iPad compatibility, as well as onboard control of Roland SuperNATURAL-powered synths. You get robust performance control with assignable knobs and switches, octave and transpose buttons, keyboard split and layer functions, sustain and expression pedal inputs, and Roland's bend/mod lever and D-BEAM controller.

Figure 2.11 Roland A-88.

VIDEO 2.4 ROLAND A-88 AND A-49.

Figure 2.12
http://youtu.be/614K-P6nu_4

Step 2: What You Need to Connect the MIDI Keyboard to Your iPad

After you have selected a type of MIDI keyboard, you should review what is needed in order for the device to connect to your iPad. The options include the following:

1. Some keyboards, such as the iRig KEYS with Lightning, do not need any other devices, as they connect directly to the iPad via the Lightning or 30-pin connector.
2. If the keyboard is iOS class compliant (the majority of the keyboards listed in this chapter), then you will need the **Apple Camera Connector Kit**, which adds a USB input, and you connect the keyboard's USB cable directly to your iPad.

3. If you have an older MIDI keyboard that does not have USB or direct connection to the iPad (none of which are listed in this chapter), then you will need to purchase a MIDI interface that connects to the iPad as well as the keyboard's MIDI in and out ports.

Where's the USB Port?

If the MIDI keyboard you have selected must be connected to the iPad via USB, you will need to purchase an adapter, as the iPad does not have a USB port.

Class Compliant Device

A class compliant device is one that doesn't require drivers to be installed in order to connect to a Windows or Macintosh computer, or to your iPad. Class compliant devices use drivers that are already built into the operating system of the device (computer or iPad). To find out if your USB audio or MIDI device is class compliant, check the manufacturer's web page. The keyboards listed in this chapter are all class compliant.

The following options are for connecting one MIDI keyboard directly to your iPad. For connecting multiple MIDI devices, refer to chapter 6.

Apple Camera Connection Kit

The cable that came with your iPad, which is designed to connect your iPad to your Mac or Windows computer, can't be used to connect MIDI gear. The reason is that the USB plug is designed to plug into a female USB port on your Mac or Windows computer (see chapter 1).

The Apple Camera Connection Kit connects to the iPad port and makes it possible to connect to it via the USB port that is part of the kit. It was originally designed for connecting cameras, but since it is a USB port, it will work with MIDI gear that does not require drivers to be installed.

For iPads that use the 30-pin connector, the Apple Camera Connection Kit comes in two different configurations: one is a USB port, and the other is an SD card reader to import photos, audio, and videos directly from a camera or audio device SD card: http://store.apple.com/us/product/MC531ZM/A/apple-ipad-camera-connection-kit.

Figure 2.13 Apple Camera Connection Kit with 30-pin connector.

For iPads that use the Lightning connector (see chapter 1), you should purchase the Lightning to USB Camera Connector. This item is only one cable. If you want to import SD card data, you will have to purchase a separate device: http://store.apple.com/us/product/MD822ZM/A/lightning-to-sd-card-camera-reader.

Figure 2.14. Apple Camera Connection Kit
Lightning to USB Connector.

Apple Camera Connection Kit Clones

There are Apple Camera Connection Kit clones available, but they are not supported by Apple and are not receiving consistent positive reviews from users. Therefore, I don't recommend these devices. If you do a search on Amazon or eBay for "iPad camera connection kit," you will get a variety of hits. The advantage to these devices is that they are very inexpensive and include several connectors on one kit. If you do try this route, be sure you can return the item if it does not work with your iPad.

When you plug in one of these clones, you may get a message: "this accessory is not supported by this iPad." However, when I clicked OK, the MIDI device did work. Therefore, the results can be intermittent.

Extender Cables

One of the problems when connecting the Apple Camera Connector to your iPad is that the device hangs out of the side of the iPad. The weight of an Apple Camera Connector and the tension of connecting a device tends to pull the Camera Connection Kit adapter out of the dock connector and put stress on the connector.

In order to alleviate this, you can purchase a dock extension cable that runs between the Camera Connection Kit adapter and the dock connector on the iPad. As of this writing, Apple does not sell a product, so check the ratings to be sure that the cable works with your iPad and devices. Some of the third-party connectors do not work properly. One of the best options is the Cablejive dockXtender: www.cablejive .com/products/dockXtender.html.

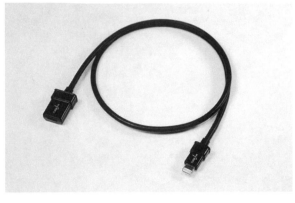

Figure 2.15. Cablejive connector extension cable.

VIDEO 2.5 CONNECTING THE APPLE CAMERA
CONNECTION KIT WITH MIDI GEAR.

Figure 2.16
http://youtu.be/AzLapwA0TGQ

MIDI Connectors

The next-best option for connecting a MIDI keyboard or device is to use an interface designed for this specific use. There are advantages, as the devices have more features than just a USB input, as is the case with the Apple Camera Connection Kit cable. The cost is somewhat higher than the Apple Camera Connection Kit, but the advantages are worth the investment.

30-Pin to Lightning Adapter ($39.95)

As of this writing, the MIDI connectors are 30-pin, designed for the iPad 2 and iPads that were produced with 30-pin connectors. In the future, there will surely be options that come with Lightning connectors. However, 30-pin connectors can be used via a 30-pin to Lightning connector. The advantage to purchasing this item is that it also acts as an extender, so you will not need to purchase a cable extender as described earlier in this chapter. The Apple item is 0.2 meters or approximately 8 inches long: http://store.apple.com/us/product/MD824ZM/A/lightning-to-30-pin-adapter-02-m.

Figure 2.17.

VIDEO 2.6. CONNECTING 30-PIN MIDI IOS
DEVICES TO LIGHTNING CONNECTORS.

Figure 2.18
http://vimeo.com/87736658

iRig MIDI ($69.95 list)
www.ikmultimedia.com/products/irigmidi/

The iRig MIDI is a 30-pin MIDI interface that connects to your iPad via a 30-pin connector or with the Apple 30-pin to Lightning connector. The interface connects to the MIDI device via the MIDI out and in ports on the instrument. This allows the iRig MIDI to work with any MIDI device with a 5-pin DIN MIDI connector. The iRig MIDI will *not* work with MIDI devices that only connect to the iPad via USB.

Figure 2.19. MIDI ports.

In addition to the interface, the price includes two excellent apps for the iPad produced by IK Multimedia, Sample Tank (A $5.99 stand-alone app, mentioned in chapter 3 [page 66] of the *Musical iPad*) and a MIDI recorder app. For more information on the apps, refer to the IK Multimedia website. The interface will work with other apps such as GarageBand and Cubasis.

iRig MIDI includes 3 MIDI ports: IN, OUT, and THRU. These connect to any standard MIDI jacks using the included 2 x 1.6 meter/5.2-inch cables. iRig MIDI also has two LEDs for displaying the MIDI activity on the IN and OUT ports. iRig MIDI also exclusively provides a micro USB port with an included cable that connects to any standard USB power supply source, so that the iPad stays fully powered during long recording sessions.

Figure 2.20. iRig MIDI.

VIDEO 2.7. IRIG MIDI.

Figure 2.21
http://youtu.be/uOmpvSXu58k

iPad Stands

What more could you ask for? How about a place to tee up your iPad so you can actually play your instrument? Now that you are ready to scan all your music and consign those massive fake books to a box in the attic, you'll need something to hold the music at the proper height and angle while you play. There are many stands and cases already available, and new products appear on the market as more uses for the iPad take it into new environments.

The iPad Smart Cover (see chapter 1) is the stand/case combination most will be familiar with, but it favors landscape (sideways) orientation, and most music pages are formatted for portrait (tall) viewing. Most musicians will prefer one of the options designed specifically for musicians.

iKlip Studio ($29.99)

www.ikmultimedia.com/products/iklipstudio/

If your setup, or workspace, has room for a desktop stand, the iKlip from IK Multimedia can hold the iPad in either portrait or landscape orientation. The angle is adjustable, and the iKlip folds flat for easy packing and transport. If you use the same manufacturer's iRig, there is the added bonus of a detachable bracket to hold your iRig in place behind the iPad so it doesn't dangle.

Figure 2.22. iKlip Studio.

Desktop stands are also available by other computer accessory makers such as Griffin, Targus, and Belkin.

Joy Factory Tournez Retractable Clamp Mount ($149.95)

www.thejoyfactory.com/product/aab106

If desk space is at a premium, a clamp mount stand such as the Joy Factory Tournez Retractable Clamp Mount is worth considering, as it can be connected to a table and adjusted for height and visibility.

Figure 2.23. Joy Factory Tournez Retractable Clamp Mount.

Stands for Studio and Live Performance

For studio and live performance, there are a number of iPad mounts that clamp onto a mic stand and can position the iPad to be viewed in either portrait or landscape orientation. Prices are in the $40 range for this type of mount. Before purchasing, make sure to check that the bracket supports your iPad model, as there is a subtle difference in thickness between the models currently available.

K&M iPad Stands

www.k-m.de/en/

iPad Products

www.k-m.de/en/search/search/bereich/produkte?q=iPad

K&M offers a line of stands. Be careful when selecting them, as some are designed for specific iPad models. The K&M iPad 2 Mic Stand Holder ($44.99) turns the stand or boom stand into a dedicated iPad music stand.

Figure 2.24. K&M stands.

Standzout Telescoping Floor Stand ($99.95)

www.standzout.com/

If you don't have a mic stand to repurpose, Standzout offers a dedicated floor stand, but it is best suited for studio or home use, as it is not easily portable.

Figure 2.25. Standzout Floor Stand.

Ultimate Support HyperPad 5 in 1 Stand ($69.99)
www.ultimatesupport.com/product/HYP-100B

If your iPad usage fits all of the above criteria and you need something that can be used in multiple ways, consider Ultimate Support's offering. It provides the hardware for three different mountings, so you'll have everything you need to begin performing.

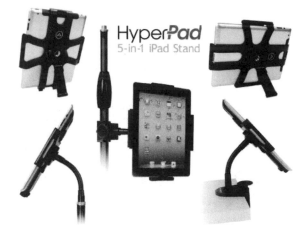

Figure 2.26. HyperPad 5 in 1 Stand.

Page Turners

In order to turn pages using an iPad, you have two options: use your hand, or purcwhase a foot pedal. Since the piano requires both hands, a foot-controlled page turner is recommended for performance and practice.

AirTurn BT105 ($119.95) (includes two footswitches)
http://airturn.com/

The AirTurn BT 105 is actually three separate pieces: a Bluetooth transmitter unit that also houses the rechargeable battery, and two footswitches for turning forward and backward. The footswitches are "mechanism free" devices for silent operation in acoustic settings, such as in-the-studio recording or live concerts. The battery is capable of 100 hours of operation and is charged via USB. The device can be used with computers as well as the iPad. AirTurn also markets iPad stands and offers packages when both are purchased together.

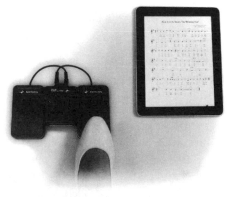

Figure 2.27. AirTurn BT105.

You can view a list of the compatible iPad apps on the AirTurn website: www.airturn.com/ipad-apps/apps/ipad-apps.

VIDEO 2.1. AIRTURN SETUP AND THE ONSONG APP.

Figure 2.28
http://youtu.be/KeqfTk1VPn4

PageFlip Cicada ($89.99)
www.pageflip.com/pageflipCicada.html

The PageFlip Cicada is a Bluetooth 3.0 device that can run on batteries or AC power. The unit has two pedals, one for forward turns and one for backward turns. The range for wireless communication is 10 meters, and with Bluetooth pairing, it is possible to control multiple units onstage or in the studio with no conflicts. The unit is also compatible with computers, so you can use it with your Bluetooth-enabled desktop or laptop machine. Before purchasing a foot-controlled page turner, check to be sure it is compatible with your apps: www.pageflip.com/app_list.html.

Figure 2.29. PageFlip Cicada.

BT-2/BT-4 Bluetooth MIDI Foot Controllers by Positive Grid ($99.99 for the BT-4 four-button set and $79.99 for the BT-2 two-button set)
www.positivegrid.com/bt4/

Positive Grid's BT-2 and BT-4 foot controllers are MIDI foot controllers based on Bluetooth 4.0 technology. They allow users to assign MIDI messages to the controllers by using an iOS app that edits the assignments. Each and every MIDI-compatible iOS app supports a standard communication protocol that enables it to be controlled wirelessly.

These apps can be from the Positive Grid family of products, including JamUp XT and JamUp Pro XT (see chapter 3), or any other MIDI-compatible app or desktop software, such as GarageBand, OnSong, and Auria. Both BT pedals can be expanded by adding an expression pedal or footswitch using a 1/4-inch phone-type jack, allowing musicians to control rotary functions like whammy and wah effects, keyboard sustain, amp gain and volume, EQ, and more. Products will be available in 2014.

Figure 2.30. Bluetooth MIDI Foot Controllers.

MIDI Studio Options

Below are several options for a MIDI studio where you are connecting a single MIDI keyboard directly to your iPad. These are sample configurations. Be sure to review the entire chapter and contact your favorite music dealer before purchasing the specific gear.

MIDI Studio 1: Low to moderate cost; portable; 26 or 37 mini-sized keys; direct connection to iPad or via the Apple Camera Connection Kit USB Connector

- iPad 2 or later: starting at $499.00
- Music app such as GarageBand ($4.99), Cubasis ($49.99), Notion ($14.99), or similar app that supports MIDI keyboard input: $4.99–$49.99
- MIDI keyboard with 25 or 37 mini keys: $125.00
- Apple Camera Connection Kit: $29.00

Total cost including iPad: $657.99–$702.99

MIDI Studio 2: Low to moderate cost; portable; 26 full-sized keys; Apple Camera Connection Kit required

- iPad 2 or later: starting at $499.00
- Music app such as GarageBand ($4.99), Cubasis ($49.99), Notion ($14.99), or similar app that supports MIDI keyboard input: $4.99–$49.99
- MIDI keyboard with 26 or 37 mini keys: $150.00
- Apple Camera Connection Kit: $29.00

Total cost including iPad: $682.99–$727.99

MIDI Studio 3: Moderate to high cost; portable; 49 or 61 full-sized keys; Apple Camera Connection Kit required

- iPad 2 or later: starting at $499.00
- Music app such as GarageBand ($4.99), Cubasis ($49.99), Notion ($14.99), or similar app that supports MIDI keyboard input: $4.99–$49.99

- MIDI keyboard with 26 or 37 mini keys: $200.00–$400.00
- Apple Camera Connection Kit: $29.00

Total cost including iPad: $732.99–$977.99

MIDI Studio 4: High cost; portable; 88 full-sized weighted keys; Apple Camera Connection Kit USB connector

- iPad 2 or later: $499.00
- Music app such as GarageBand ($4.99), Cubasis ($49.99), Notion ($14.99), or similar app that supports MIDI keyboard input: $4.99–$49.99
- MIDI keyboard with 88 full-sized weighted keys: $900.00–$2,000.00
- Apple Camera Connection Kit: $29.00

Total cost including iPad: $1,432.99–$2,577.99

MIDI Studio 5: Moderate cost; use an older MIDI keyboard that is not iOS compliant but does have MIDI IN and OUT ports; iOS MIDI adapter

- iPad 2 or later: starting at $499.00
- Music app such as GarageBand ($4.99), Cubasis ($49.99), Notion ($14.99), or similar app that supports MIDI keyboard input: $4.99–$49.99
- Use an existing MIDI Keyboard with MIDI in and out ports: no cost
- iRig MIDI or similar MIDI interface: $69.95

Total cost including iPad: $573.94–$618.94

Chapter 2 Activities

1. Select the best type of MIDI keyboard controller for your personal use and/or your studio.
2. Purchase one of the connectors mentioned in this chapter, and connect a compatible MIDI device.
3. Practice note entry with one of your music apps, such as GarageBand, Notion, or another.
4. Choose an iPad stand for your studio.
5. Select one of the sample MIDI studio options, and modify as needed.

Summary

This chapter introduced the various MIDI keyboard options that are designed to be directly connected to an iPad with a direct connection or via the Apple Camera Connection Kit or an iOS-compatible MIDI interface. The specific hardware options for connecting a single MIDI keyboard were reviewed. iPad stands were introduced for use in the music studio.

Chapter 3

ELECTRIC GUITAR AND BASS INPUT AND PROCESSING

This chapter addresses iPad applications for guitarists and bassists to enhance practice and performance. It begins with an overview of the electric guitar and bass hardware setup or rig and signal flow from instrument to speaker, and is followed by a review of essential iPad apps that emulate amps, effects, and speakers. Various options for connecting the guitar signal to the iPad and using an external pedalboard are included.

The hardware and iPad apps presented in this chapter offer guitarists and bassists the opportunity to use virtual models of effects, amps, speaker cabinets, and microphone placements to emulate the sound of classic gear at a fraction of the cost of the actual equipment. It is a cost-effective way to build a rig, and the iPad apps and gear presented in this chapter can reduce the needed hardware and provide the option to practice and "crank it up" at any time, in any location.

The Guitarist's Rig: An Overview

The iPad offers the possibility of emulating classic sounds and discovering new ones, all in a package that weighs and costs less than its hardware counterparts. Each player's sound is the result of connecting several pieces of equipment to produce a unique sound. If guitar and bass setup is new to you, read through the list below to help you understand how the iPad and apps fit into a rig. If you are familiar with the rig setup for electric guitar and bass, move to the effects apps section later in this chapter.

An Electric Guitar or Bass Tone
Is Comprised of Five Elements:

1. The instrument. There are many different models of guitars and basses, each with its own distinctive tone. The guitar's tone comes from the electronics used to pick up the vibration of the string. This is why a Fender Telecaster sounds different from a Gibson Les Paul model guitar.

2. The effects. The signal leaves the guitar via a 1/4-inch phone connector and travels via a cable through any number of effects boxes. These boxes are called stompboxes, since they are turned on and off using a footswitch. Typical effects found in stompboxes include distortion, tremolo, wah–wah, chorus, flanger, and reverb. These effects units are connected to each other in a chain with 1/4-inch cables. The footswitch controls whether the signal is processed by a particular effect, or bypassed and sent to the next effect. A volume pedal can also be added to the chain to control the output of the effected signal before it is routed to the amplifier.

3. The amplifier. This is another part of what makes up a guitarist's sound. An amplifier is used to convert the signal to a sound, and it is either a separate unit or built into the amp's speaker cabinet. The separate amp unit is called the amp head. There are many models of amp heads available, each designed to have its own unique sound. The amp head is more portable than one built into a speaker cabinet, and an amp head can be connected to any number of speaker cabinets.

4. The speaker cabinet. The last part of the guitar signal chain is the speaker cabinet. The choice of manufacturer, size, and wattage all contribute to a guitarist's sound. Speaker cabinets are available in a wide range of sizes and prices. With all equipment choices, it comes down to the style of music and what sound is the best.

5. The microphone. In the studio, a microphone is often used to pick up the sound of the amp. The position of the microphone contributes to the sound that is recorded. Both the type of microphone and its position relative to the speaker cabinet add another element of the guitar tone as it is recorded.

Now that we have reviewed the elements of what makes the electric guitar or bass sound unique, the rest of this chapter will review the way you can enhance each of these elements with apps and your iPad.

Effects Apps

The apps in this section model the sound of effects, amps, and speakers. Each app strives to provide the guitarist or bassist with the same unique sounds he or she could create with hardware. The apps in this section are a sampling of the more popular guitar and bass effects apps.

GarageBand by Apple
(free/in-app purchase upgrade for instrument sound package: $4.99)
https://itunes.apple.com/us/app/garageband/id408709785?mt=8

GarageBand has a collection of amp and stompbox emulations in the Instruments section of the app. There are nine amp emulations, from classic Fender to modern metal. You can choose up to four stompboxes from the library of ten. You can connect your guitar or bass to GarageBand using any of the interfaces listed later in this chapter. GarageBand's recording capabilities will be mentioned in chapter 7.

Figure 3.1. GarageBand amp.

VIDEO 3.1. GARAGEBAND GUITAR AMPS DEMO.

Figure 3.2.
http://youtu.be/NBG_fTgVwtg

iShred LIVE by Frontier Design Group (free/in-app purchases available)
https://itunes.apple.com/us/app/ishred-live/id375957618?mt=8

iShred LIVE focuses on virtual effects or stompbox emulations. The app offers two free effects, the Q-36 Space Modulator and HK-200 Delay Unit, along with a noise gate and an amp simulator. Other effects are priced at either $0.99 or $1.99 and are available via in-app purchase. An audio recorder is available via an in-app purchase of $2.99 that will record the app's output. A tuner, metronome, and MP3 player are also included.

Figure 3.3. iShred LIVE.

VIDEO 3.2. ISHRED LIVE DEMO.

Figure 3.4.
http://youtu.be/WbJW_1yOiks

AmpliTube for iPad by IK Multimedia
(free/in-app purchases available: $19.99)
https://itunes.apple.com/us/app/amplitube-free-for-ipad/id373743686?mt=8

AmpliTube is available in several versions:

- AmpliTube Free: A free version allowing you to try a very limited sound set before you purchase.
- AmpliTube for iPad: Includes (via in-app purchases) additional stompbox effects, amps, recorder effects, loops, bundles (such as the Fender, Slash, and Jimi Hendrix sounds), and a more advanced tuner.
- AmpliTube Fender™: A specialized version of Amplitude, consisting of Fender amp and effects emulations. This set can be purchased in the main version of AmpliTube if you want more than just the Fender emulations.
- AmpliTube Fender™ Free: A free, limited version for auditioning the app.

- AmpliTube Slash: A specialized version featuring emulations of the gear used by Guns N' Roses guitarist Slash.
- AmpliTube Jimi Hendrix™: A specialized version featuring gear used by Jimi Hendrix.
- AmpliTube LE: A version optimized for the iPhone and iPod touch.

All versions of AmpliTube support four simultaneous stompbox effects along with a virtual amp, speaker cabinet, and microphone. You can record tracks on the app's internal recorder, which can be expanded to eight tracks via an in-app purchase. You can play along with songs in your iTunes library, and use the "No Voice" feature to remove the lead vocal or guitar solo from a track.

You can export your recorded performances to SoundCloud, or use e-mail, FTP or iTunes File Sharing. AmpliTube works well with the iRig line of interfaces (discussed later in this chapter), as both are IK Multimedia products. AmpliTube can be used with other recording apps, such as GarageBand and Cubasis, using Audiobus for iPads running iOS5 or later and Inter-App Audio for iPads running iOS7 or later. See chapter 7 for more information on these features.

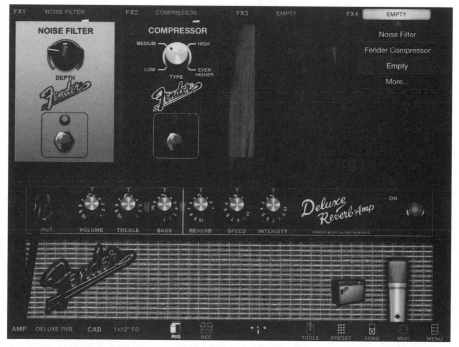

Figure 3.5. AmpliTube Fender.

VIDEO 3.3. AMPLITUBE AND IRIG DEMO.

Figure 3.6
http://youtu.be/SU11pniDa3M

AmpKit by Agile Partners (free/in-app purchases available)
https://itunes.apple.com/gb/app/ampkit/id364011231?mt=8

AmpKit was created in conjunction with the Peavey company, another storied name in the electric guitar and bass world. There are emulations of many classic amps, with special attention to Peavey's own models. The free version of AmpKit contains a single amp and a noise gate stompbox. Additional amps and effects can be added via in-app purchase. Amps and cabinets can be mixed and matched, and on newer iOS devices, up to 32 pedal effects per setup can be placed anywhere in the signal chain. Audiobus support (see chapter 7) can link your guitar or bass to any supported recording app. AmpKit will also appear in the Audiobus effects and output list so it can be used to process signals from other sources, such as a synthesizer app or microphone for vocal input. AmpKit can record your performances, and you can upload your audio files to SoundCloud, export via e-mail, or copy and paste. You can play along with any track in your iTunes library or your own original tracks.

For bass players, there are five bass amps with matching speaker cabinets in the Bass Essentials Pack, available for $17.99 in the Agile Partners online store. The Setlist feature allows you to group setups so you can move seamlessly from one to the next on a gig or in a recording session. AmpKit will run in the background, should you want to use it with Agile Partners GuitarToolkit or TabToolkit. GuitarToolkit is mentioned in chapter 7 (page 137) of the *Musical iPad*. AmpKit supports MIDI control, such as AirTurn for controlling amps and pedals, and Setlist navigation.

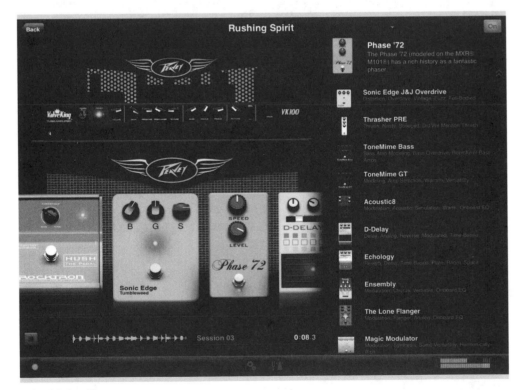

Figure 3.7. AmpKit.

VIDEO 3.4. AMPKIT DEMO.

Figure 3.8
http://youtu.be/H61LW73immc

GuitarTone by Sonoma Wire Works (in-app purchases available: $2.99)
https://itunes.apple.com/us/app/guitartone/id418093519?mt=8

GuitarTone has a few features that make it unique and worthy of investigation. Amp heads, speaker cabinets, and effects are each organized neatly in their own section of the screen. Visually, it is designed to work in iPad portrait mode. To select a new piece of gear, swipe horizontally in each section, and available gear will slide into view. On all iPad models, you can emulate stereo speaker cabinets, which can be either the same cabinet or a mix of cabinets for a fatter tone. Each cabinet can have its own choice of virtual microphone for additional tone variation. Up to three stompboxes can be used at a time, and combinations of effects can be saved as presets on the pedalboard at the bottom of the screen. Should you want to use the pedal effects with your own amp and cabinet, you can bypass the software amp and cabinet and send the output of your iPad to the physical amp, via either the headphone jack or the GuitarJack interface mentioned later in this chapter. There is a noise gate to filter out unwanted noise.

Audiobus (see chapter 7) is supported for both the input and effects sections, so you can use the GuitarTone app to process signals from another app or external sound source. GuitarTone has no internal recording capability, but if that is a feature you want, check out StudioTrack from Sonoma Wire Works, available for $9.99. StudioTrack is a multitrack recording app that happens to have GuitarTone built in, so you can get the features of both for a single price. Using StudioTrack with GuitarJack will give you access to a bonus collection of amps and effects when the app and the interface are connected.

Figure 3.9. GuitarTone.

VIDEO 3.5. GUITARTONE DEMO.

Figure 3.10.
http://youtu.be/t1x6eZUfshc

DigiTech Stomp Shop by Harmon Professional Inc. (free/in-app purchases available)

https://itunes.apple.com/us/app/digitech-stomp-shop/id481957668?mt=8

The DigiTech Stomp Shop app is the companion to DigiTech's iStomp pedal, which is mentioned later in this chapter. The app is a gateway to an online shop where you can purchase and download effects pedal apps. The app works only with DigiTech's hardware.

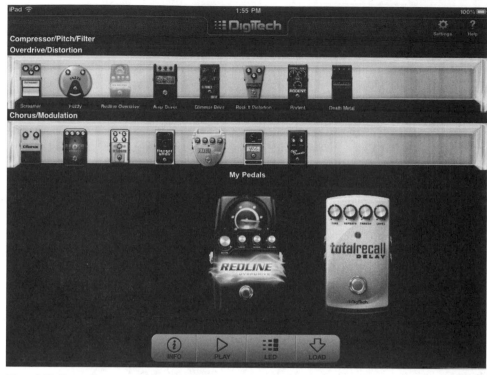

Figure 3.11. Stomp Shop.

VIDEO 3.6. STOMP SHOP DEMO.

Figure 3.12
http://youtu.be/igbWYOYohX8

JamUp XT—Multi Effects Processor by Positive Grid Inc. (free/in-app purchases available)

https://itunes.apple.com/us/app/jamup-xt-multi-effects-processor/id449820506?mt=8

JamUp XT contains a full range of guitar effects and amps, and a store where you can expand your collection. Additional options are available through ToneSharing, an online database of artist and user presets that can be shared and downloaded. Audio output can be sent to other applications via Audiobus. Audiobus also allows the audio output from other apps to be processed through JamUp's effects with the option of being recorded by its recorder.

VIDEO 3.7. JAMUP XT WITH AUDIOBUS.

Figure 3.13
https://vimeo.com/87882266

JamUp XT is compatible with most guitar input devices, pedal effects, and controllers, such as those covered later in this chapter. In the app's Settings menu, you can enable MIDI control assignments, allowing external controllers and pedals to send MIDI controller data to JamUp. There is also a built-in tuner and metronome. With JamUpXT you can jam to any track in your iTunes library and use time stretching to change the key or tempo without affecting pitch.

Figure 3.14. JamUp XT.

VIDEO 3.8. JAMUP XT DEMO.

Figure 3.15
http://youtu.be/tVei7uTrijc

Bias—Amps! By Positive Grid Inc. ($19.99)

https://itunes.apple.com/us/app/bias-amps!/id711314889?mt=8

Bias—Amps! offers a different approach to the amp emulation model. In addition to the amp and speaker emulations and mic placement options, Bias—Amps! allows you to design and save your own custom amps. There are amps for both guitar and bass players. Your amplifier creations can be transferred to JamUp XT, where you can add some effects pedals. You can also take advantage of the eight-track recorder for songwriting or looping. Bias supports Audiobus and Inter-App Audio, so it works with GarageBand, Cubasis, and Auria (see chapter 7).

Positive Grid also hosts ToneCloud, a platform for Bias–Amps! users to share their creations with each other. Bias—Amps! is designed to integrate with JamUp XT, mentioned previously in this chapter.

Figure 3.16. Bias–Amps!

VIDEO 3.9. BIAS–AMPS! DEMO.

Figure 3.17
http://youtu.be/atZTQSVz_X8

Tip: Apps that include amp and effects emulators, tuners, and recording capability can save you money by having an all-in-one app solution for a variety of needs. However, don't overlook the features of specialized apps for each task, as some dedicated apps offer more options.

Connecting the Guitar or Bass Output to the iPad

To utilize the power of the apps mentioned previously in this chapter, you need a way to connect the output of your guitar or bass to the iPad. This is done via an interface or A/D (analog to digital) converter. There are many different options from which to choose, and there are specific features you will want to consider, such as audio quality and inclusion of a headphone jack. In some recording situations, the speaker is bypassed by using a direct input box, or *DI*. This device converts the signal to line level for recording only the sound of the guitar, effects, and amp. Some guitarists find that using one of the interfaces in the following section feels similar to using a direct box.

> **Tip:** The devices listed in this section perform the task of digitizing the signal from your guitar and routing it to the input of the selected app. Since these devices are A/D (analog to digital) converters, the sampling rate and resolution of each unit is important to consider if you plan use your iPad for recording. Interfaces that have 44.1 kHz/16-bit resolution are acceptable, but 48 kHz/24-bit or higher is preferred. Higher resolution in digital audio is much like pixels for digital cameras: the higher the number, the greater the detail that is captured. Be sure to compare the features and extras of each unit as well, such as software that is bundled with the purchase.

GuitarConnect Cable Premium by Griffin ($29.99)
http://store.griffintechnology.com/guitarconnect-cable

GuitarConnect is a six-foot-long cable that connects your guitar directly to the iPad. A stereo 1/8-inch jack connects to the iPad's headphone jack. On the other end is a 1/4-inch jack for connecting the guitar's output and a 1/8-inch jack for connecting headphones. GuitarConnect is compatible with the iPad 2 and newer models, including the iPad Mini.

Figure 3.18. GuitarConnect Cable Premium.

VIDEO 3.10. GUITARCONNECT DEMO.

Figure 3.19
http://youtu.be/WbJW_1yOiks

JamUp Plug by Positive Grid ($39.99 list price)
www.positivegrid.com/jamup-plug/

JamUp Plug connects through the iPad's headphone jack. The plug's simple design has an input jack for the guitar or bass, and an output connection for headphones or for connecting to a mixer or amp. It is compatible with iOS5 or later.

Figure 3.20. JamUp Plug.

iRig by IK Multimedia ($39.99 list price)
www.ikmultimedia.com/products/irig/

AmpliTube iRig is an A/D converter and comes with the AmpliTube free iOS app mentioned previously in this chapter. It connects to the iPad through the headphone jack. The advantage to having the device connect to the headphone jack is that the 30-pin or Lightning port is free to connect to the charger, so battery life is not a factor when using the iRig. This also makes the iRig compatible with both 30-pin and Lightning models of the iPad. There is a 1/4-inch jack to connect your guitar, bass, or other electronic instrument and a 1/8-inch jack for connecting headphones. The connection is low-latency, which means there may be a small, detectable delay from the pluck of the string until the sound is heard in the headphones. Though the iRig is designed for use with acoustic and electric guitars and basses, it does work with a keyboard synthesizer and mixer input as well.

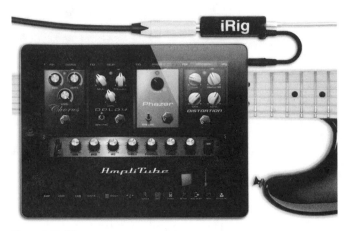

Figure 3.21. iRig.

VIDEO 3.11. IRIG DEMO.

Figure 3.22
http://youtu.be/rZa1QOcCptA

iRig HD by IK Multimedia ($99.99 list price)
www.ikmultimedia.com/products/irighd/

iRig HD is an updated and more expensive version of the iRig that offers upgrades in its preamp and A/D converter. The preamp takes the incoming signal and raises it to line level for further processing—in this case by the A/D converter, which converts the signal into digital format for the iPad's apps to process. iRig HD supports both 44.1 and 48 kHz sampling rates and 24-bit resolution. It also comes with a USB cable to connect to a Mac or PC computer.

Figure 3.23. iRig HD.

VIDEO 3.12. IRIG HD DEMO.

Figure 3.24
http://youtu.be/QHJRu4UAN1A

iRig PRO by IK Multimedia ($149.99 list price)

www.ikmultimedia.com/products/irigpro/

The pocket-sized iRig PRO is an audio interface that can be used with iOS devices and Mac or PC computers. It has a 1/4-inch XLR combo jack that can receive a guitar/bass or a microphone, and it has switchable 48-volt power for condenser mics (see chapter 5). iRig PRO's preamp and 24-bit A/D converter provide a clean digital audio signal. It also has an adjustable gain (volume) control. The iRig PRO also functions as a MIDI interface, so you can connect a MIDI keyboard (see chapter 2).

Figure 3.25. iRig PRO.

VIDEO 3.13. IRIG PRO DEMO.

Figure 3.26
http://youtu.be/IIq1XQPVGC0

GuitarConnect Pro by Griffin ($89.99)

http://store.griffintechnology.com/guitarconnect-pro

GuitarConnect Pro is an interface for connecting a guitar, bass, or keyboard to your iPad. Cables are provided to accommodate either 30-pin or Lightning iPad connections. The device is bus powered, meaning it draws power through the cable connected to the iPad, so there is no power cable or battery required. You can control the volume of the input from the guitar; output is monitored via the iPad's headphone jack. GuitarConnect Pro can also be used with a Mac computer, via the supplied USB cable.

Figure 3.27. GuitarConnect Pro.

VIDEO 3.14. GUITARCONNECT PRO DEMO.

Figure 3.28
http://youtu.be/rF3QroU6ppc

JAM by Apogee Digital ($99)

www.apogeedigital.com/products/jam.php

JAM, like the other interfaces mentioned in this chapter, is designed to work specifically with a guitar or bass. It is compatible with iPad models running iOS 4.3 or later using either a 30-pin or Lightning connector. There are two connections: one to the guitar or bass, and one to the iPad or computer. The LED (light-emitting diode) turns blue to indicate a connection, green to indicate it is ready to work, and red to indicate the gain level is too high. There is a wheel on the side of JAM to adjust the gain higher or lower. JAM supports recording up to 48 kHz/24-bit resolution.

Figure 03.29. JAM.

VIDEO 3.15. JAM DEMO.

Figure 3.30
http://youtu.be/RkL0blx-ESk

Sonic Port by Line 6 ($139.95)
http://line6.com/sonicport/

Sonic Port has the advantage of being made by a company that also makes guitars, amps, and effects. It works with all iPad models. It comes with both 30-pin and Lightning cables. The unit has two 1/8-inch stereo jacks, one in and one out, and two 1/4-inch stereo jacks, one in and one out. This provides the flexibility for routing multiple instruments into the Sonic Port for recording, and running multiple outs for monitoring live performance and practicing. For recording, resolutions up to 48 kHz/24-bit are supported. Sonic Port can be used with GarageBand or other iOS recording apps (see chapter 7).

Sonic Port comes with the Mobile POD app, an effect and amp emulation package that includes an extensive library of effects combinations. You can create and save your own effects settings and combinations as well. The app includes an MP3 player so you can jam with your tracks. A tuner is also included, so there is no need to change apps to tune.

> **Tip:** Anyone using Sonic Port with Jammit (this app is mentioned in chapter 9 [page 172] of *Musical iPad*), the app that allows you to record a part on many classic rock tracks, will benefit from a feature that unlocks Line 6 effects that fit the part you are performing on the guitar tracks you purchase in the Jammit library. Jammit is a free app, with in-app purchases of individual songs available.

Figure 3.31. Sonic Port.

VIDEO 3.16. SONIC PORT DEMO.

Figure 3.32
http://youtu.be/WXqrnLnm-T0

iJam by RapcoHorizon ($99)

www.rapcohorizon.com/p-618-ijam.aspx

iJam is a practice assistant, allowing you to mix your guitar's output with the output of the iPad and play along, monitoring the sound with headphones. There are two connections: a 1/4-inch jack for the guitar or bass, and a 1/8-inch stereo cable for the iPad. A 9-volt battery is required to power the unit. There are three ways to use iJam:

1. As an iPad guitar interface.
2. As a practice amplifier with the guitar or bass connected, using headphones for monitoring.
3. As an MP3 play-along device, using any MP3 player. Connect the MP3 player using a 1/8-inch stereo cable, and you can play along with any track to practice, learn parts, or work out song ideas.

Figure 3.33. iJam.

VIDEO 3.17. IJAM DEMO.

Figure 3.34
http://youtu.be/G9jezZJt1ek

GuitarJack Model 2 by Sonoma Wire Works ($199 list price)
www.sonomawireworks.com/guitarjack/

GuitarJack Model 2 is an interface for guitar or bass that attaches directly to the iPad via the 30-pin port. If you have an iPad with a Lightning input, you will need to purchase Apple's Lightning to 30-pin adapter cable (see chapter 1). The unit accepts three jacks: a 1/4-inch cable from the guitar or bass, a 1/8-inch headphone jack, and a 1/8-inch microphone jack.

GuitarJack works with multitrack recording apps (see chapter 7) and other apps listed in this chapter, including Amplitude for iPad and JamUP XT. However, there is added value in using Sonoma Wire Works' GuitarTone app, mentioned previously in this chapter. The interface adds additional GuitarTone amps and effects to your online store account free of charge. The extra tones are also available in FourTrack and StudioTrack multitrack recording apps for iOS devices. Sonoma Wire Works also makes TaylorEQ, a free app that enhances the tone of Taylor guitars when used with the interface.

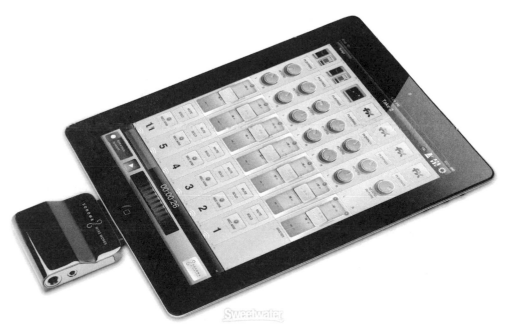

Figure 3.35. GuitarJack.

VIDEO 3.18. GUITARJACK DEMO.

Figure 3.36
http://youtu.be/MVJZAx3uvXY

Ampkit Link HD by Peavey (159.99 list price)

www.peavey.com/products/ampkitlink/

Ampkit Link HD is designed to be used with the Ampkit app mentioned previously in this chapter. Ampkit contains a collection of emulations of classic Peavey amps. Ampkit Link HD provides connections to the iPad using either 30-pin or Lightning connectors. There is a 1/4-inch input jack for guitar or bass, a 1/8-inch headphone jack, and an output jack for sending the signal to an amp or mixer. Ampkit Link HD has a jack for an optional AC adapter to keep your iPad charged while you play. There are two control knobs, one for input gain and the other for headphone level. The unit has a rubberized coating to keep it from sliding or vibrating off of any surface.

Figure 3.37. Ampkit Link HD.

VIDEO 3.19. PEAVEY AMPKIT LINK HD DEMO.

Figure 3.38
http://youtu.be/foUqXXTxnaw

Effects Hardware

When playing or recording live, guitar and bass parts typically have very little time to change sounds or effects. Enter the stompbox, an effects processor that has knobs for tweaking and, most importantly, a foot switch to turn it on and off while playing.

StompBox by Griffin ($49.99)

http://www.sweetwater.com/store/detail/StompBox/

The Griffin StompBox is a four-switch pedalboard designed to work with all of the apps listed previously in this chapter. Its hardware compatibility as of this writing is limited to iPads with a 30-pin port. The unit draws power from its connection to the iPad, so no power cable is required. Griffin features compatibility with the JamUp app, in which an icon appears when it detects the connection to StompBox. Assigning a switch on the StompBox to a switch in an app is done from inside the app. StompBox has a single 1/4-inch jack on the rear panel for connecting an expression or volume pedal.

Figure 3.39. StompBox.

VIDEO 3.20. STOMPBOX DEMO.

Figure 3.40
http://youtu.be/lTVXQLkP7WA

iRig Stomp by IK Multimedia ($59.99)

www.ikmultimedia.com/products/irigstomp/

iRig Stomp is a hardware switch and controller that works with IK Multimedia's AmpliTube app, as well as any other guitar processing software apps that use the iPad's headphone jack, such as iShred. The interface portion of Stomp is based on the iRig interface, so it connects through the iPad headphone jack. It is powered by a 9-volt battery. It can also be on a pedalboard with other effects boxes. There is a switch to bypass the iPad's output, and the gain knob will control the signal level going to the amp or other effects. iRig Stomp has a 1/8-inch headphone jack on the back panel for use while practicing.

Figure 3.41. iRig Stomp.

VIDEO 3.21. IRIG STOMP DEMO.

Figure 3.42
http://youtu.be/icCgDk3apHU

iRig BlueBoard by IK Multimedia ($99.99)
www.ikmultimedia.com/products/irigblueboard/

iRig BlueBoard is a wireless controller that communicates with the iPad via Bluetooth. Communication with the iPad is managed by the iRig BlueBoard app. BlueBoard requires four AAA batteries that power it and the LEDs that illuminate the buttons when active. It has a communication range of 10 meters, a little over 32 feet. There are two 1/4-inch jacks on the side for connecting expression or volume pedals.

Though primarily a pedalboard, BlueBoard is designed to work with the AmpliTube app family and other guitar effects apps such as Ampkit and JamUp XT. BlueBoard can work with a variety of other apps that accept MIDI messages, such as NLogSynth Pro, SampleTank, OnSong, and VocaLive. You can change presets or patches, or toggle effects on and off.

Figure 3.43. iRig BlueBoard.

VIDEO 3.22. IRIG BLUEBOARD DEMO.

Figure 3.44
http://youtu.be/iAUSvQfCuN0

Tip: Wireless communication is subject to dropouts, and once connection is restored, apps must be manually reconfigured. In other words, they don't reset and resume communication on their own. Assess the risks of using wireless communication, and be prepared to deal with dropouts.

DigiTech iStomp 3 Pack ($299.99)

www.digitech.com/en-US/products/istomp-3-pack

DigiTech iStomp is designed to emulate a stompbox, including four physical knobs on top of the unit. You can use the iStomp with the DigiTech Stomp Shop app, mentioned earlier in this chapter, to access pedal effects. The advantage to iStomp is that each stompbox can be reloaded with any virtual pedal in your collection. In the studio, you can use a different virtual pedal setup based on each track you are recording. In order to install each iStomp effect, you must connect the iPad to the pedal using the provided proprietary cable and complete the download. All purchased virtual pedals are saved in the iStomp Shop library, so you will always have access to them. Included with the iStomp pedals are adhesive labels, so you can label each pedal with the virtual effect stored on it. The iStomp connects via 1/4-inch cables, just like any other stompbox. The four knobs at the top of the box are assigned to parameters according to each virtual pedal's needs. Each iStomp requires a 9-volt battery for power. A unique feature of the iStomp Shop app is the five-minute audition period for new pedal software before you purchase, so you can hear it in the context of the rest of your setup.

Figure 3.45. iStomp 3 Pack.

VIDEO 3.23. ISTOMP DEMO.

Figure 3.46
http://youtu.be/8Q-PwEUBr8M

BT-2/BT-4 Bluetooth MIDI Foot Controllers by Positive Grid (BT-4 four-button set: $99.99/BT-2 two-button set: $79.99)
www.positivegrid.com/bt4/

The BT-2 and BT-4 are stompbox-like foot controllers designed to integrate with Positive Grid's JamUp XT and JamUp Xt Pro apps, creating a complete rig for guitar. The unit has a jack for connecting an expression pedal for the Dunlop Cry Baby effect (which imitates the sound of a muted trumpet) and the wah-wah effect. The BT-2 and BT-4 transmit MIDI messages for Bank Change, Program Change, and Control Change, and can work with apps such as Ampkit.

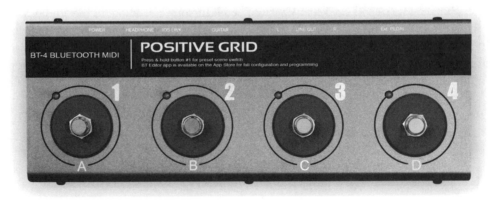

Figure 3.47. BT-4 Bluetooth MIDI Foot Controller.

AirTurn BT105 on Pedal Board with 4 ATFS 2 Pedals ($159)
http://airturn.com/

Though not a dedicated guitar pedal, AirTurn (see chapter 2) can add wireless control to JamUp XT and Ampkit Pro. AirTurn connects wirelessly with the iPad via Bluetooth. The four AirTurn pedals can function as stompbox switches, turning virtual effects off and on, or control preset changes for virtual pedals or amps.

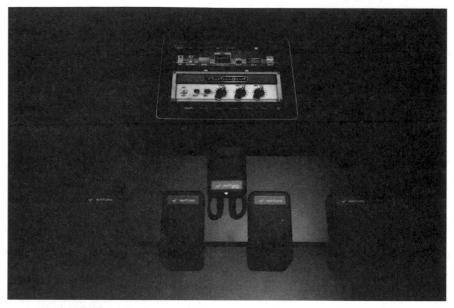

Figure 3.48. Air Turn BT105.

VIDEO 3.24 AIR TURN WITH JAMUP XT DEMO.

Figure 3.49
http://youtu.be/jTrvknb38XM

Interview with guitarist Jack Klotz Jr.

Since neither author of this book plays guitar, we called on guitarist and engineer Jack Klotz Jr. to test drive some of the software. Jack connected a Fender Telecaster through the Apogee JAM interface and auditioned the free versions of AmpliTube, AmpliTube Fender, and JamUp XT, and the full version of GarageBand.

VIDEO 3.25. JACK KLOTZ JR. INTERVIEW.

Figure 3.50
http://vimeo.com/87882136

Ergonomics

When configuring your iPad-based studio, the positioning of your equipment is just as important as the gear itself. The iPad is a hands-on interface, so you'll want to keep it within an arm's length. If you are inadvertently pushing it across a table when touching the screen, consider purchasing a different case, or a stand to keep it stationary (see chapter 2). If you read a little briskly through the keyboard chapter (and who could blame you), return and check out the section on music stands.

Connecting your equipment and interfaces with adequate cable length is another part of the equation. Instrument cables should be long enough that normal movement doesn't tug on any of the hardware and short enough that you are not walking, tripping, or rolling (office chair castors, for example) over the cable. Try to keep power cables away from any foot traffic areas.

Guitar Studio Options

Providing purchasing options is difficult, due to the various options for in-app purchases with some apps. In the sample studios below, the recording software is limited to GarageBand, as an in-app purchase of the sounds and amp emulations is only $4.99. Purchasing more powerful recording apps (see chapter 7) will increase the overall cost.

Guitar Studio Option 1

This setup combines JamUp XT with the Griffin/StompBox, and includes the 8-Track Recorder option available via in-app purchase.

- iPad 2 or later: starting at $499.00
- JamUp interface: $39.99
- JamUp XT: $9.99
- 8-Track Recorder Expansion Pack: $4.99
- Griffin StompBox: $49.99

Total cost including iPad: $603.96

Guitar Studio Option 2

This collection features IK Multimedia gear and takes advantage of the AmpliTube free app to get started. GarageBand is used for an additional sound source and as a recorder.

- iPad 2 or later: Starting at $499.00
- iRig interface: $39.99 (Includes AmpliTube free app)
- GarageBand instruments package: $4.99
- iRig Stomp: $59.99

Total cost including iPad: $603.97

Guitar Studio Option 3

This package features the Peavey sound and uses GarageBand for recording.

- iPad 2 or later: Starting at $499.00
- Peavey AmpKit Link: $159.99
- AmpKit: free
- GarageBand: free with iPad purchase

Total cost including iPad: $667.98

Guitar Studio Option 4

This collection features Sonoma Wire Works and uses the StudioTrack app that combines recording capabilities with their GuitarTone app for guitar effects processing.

- iPad 2 or later: starting at $499.00
- GuitarJack Model 2: $199.00 list price
- StudioTrack Software (contains the GuitarTone app): $9.99
- Griffin StompBox: $49.99

Total cost including iPad: $757.98

Guitar Studio Option 5

For the adventuring guitarist, create your own amp with Bias-Amps!, combine that with DigiTech stompbox sounds, and record with GarageBand.

- iPad 2 or later: starting at $499.00
- JAM interface: $99.99
- Bias-Amps!: $14.99
- DigiTech iStomp 3-Pack: $299.95 (software app is free)
- GarageBand: free with iPad purchase

Total cost including iPad: $913.93

Chapter 3 Activities

1. Download GarageBand and purchase the $4.99 instruments package. Open a new file and use the guitar or bass instrument. Then experiment with the effects that are built into the app.
2. If you own a guitar or bass interface, download a free app, such as one of the following, and audition it.
- AmpliTube Free
- AmpliTube Fender™ Free
- AmpKit
- JamUp XT
- iShred LIVE
3. Download several of the free apps listed in activity No. 2. Then go to each app's online store and calculate the number and price of all the available amps and effects that interest you. Finally, calculate the actual total cost for each app.
4. Select one of the Guitar Studio options in this chapter that best suits your personal needs. Make any modifications to it as needed.

Summary

In this chapter, we looked at iPad tools available for guitar and bass players. There are interfaces that connect a guitar or bass to the iPad to access apps for recording, effects processing, and amp and speaker cabinet emulation. There are pedals and stompboxes that connect with apps to run virtual effects that afford guitarists the same ease of use in performance that they have using conventional hardware. There are many choices available, and some free versions of apps that allow you to try before you buy. It is even possible to access many of the guitar effects and amps via Audiobus for use with any audio recorded by the iPad.

Chapter 4
DJ APPS AND GEAR

This chapter focuses on using the iPad as the main component of a DJ setup, including DJ apps for DJ production needs as well as augmenting the setup to include other gear connected to your iPad. The chapter also addresses iPad-specific mixers, mixers with platters, headphones, and speakers. It starts with the simplest and moves to the more complex DJ setup, with the iPad as the central component. iPad DJ apps have made the transition from novelty items to realistic music making, so you can use the iPad as the central component of your DJ system and create sets, record custom mixes, and more. If you are a seasoned DJ or a DJ wannabe, this chapter will get you up and running using your iPad. See chapter 8, which includes a section on using the iPad as a reinforcement to computer-based DJ rigs.

DJ Apps

There are a growing number of iPad DJ apps, allowing you to control all of your DJ needs from the device. Whether you want to create a dance mix for a party or use them as the main tool for a live event, the cost of these apps makes them a no-brainer investment.

djay 2 by Algoriddim ($9.99)
https://itunes.apple.com/us/app/djay-2/id669196929?mt=8

One of the most popular DJ apps in its second generation (djay 2) is completely rewritten for iOS and includes a powerful sampler, improved library, real grooves on the virtual vinyl, and much more. It requires iOS6, so it will not work with the older iPad models. The power and cost of this app make it appealing to both amateurs and pros. It can support a wide variety of DJ controllers. The djay 2 app lets you record any mix as an uncompressed stereo AIFF file, which iTunes can copy back to your Mac or PC and convert into an MP3—perfect for uploading your DJ sets to MixCloud.

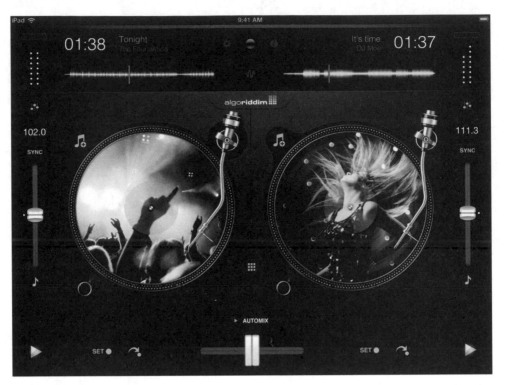

Figure 4.1. djay 2.

VIDEO 4.1 DJAY 2 DEMO.

Figure 4.2
http://youtu.be/0kTHg9GYWS0

> **Tip:** Get started for free with djay LE by Algoriddim: https://itunes.apple.com/us /app/djay-le-the-dj-app-for-ipad/id585235310?mt=8. It requires iOS6 or later, has a lot of excellent features, and you can't beat the price: free.

Traktor DJ by Native Instruments ($9.99)
https://itunes.apple.com/us/app/id592052832?mt=8

Traktor DJ includes a professional mixing system for the iPad. Uses include creating set lists and for DJ performances. It is powerful enough to replace a laptop computer in the DJ setup.

Features include creating grooves using familiar iPad swipe and pinch gestures, and familiar DJ mixer layout with cross-fader, 3-band EQ, and filter on each channel. You can access your iTunes music library directly. Use the specially designed DJ cable (discussed later in this chapter) to get up and running with your iPad and Traktor DJ.

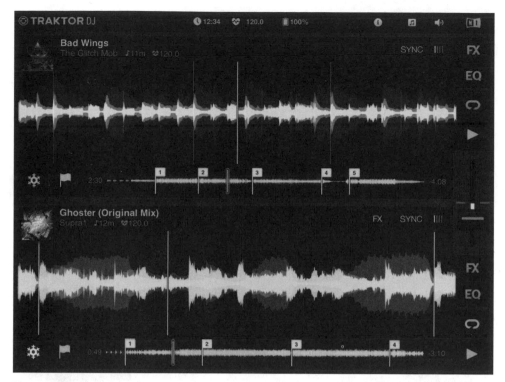

Figure 4.3 Traktor DJ.

VIDEO 4.2 TRAKTOR DJ DEMO.

Figure 4.4
http://youtu.be/i5OZGtHZz_E

You can subscribe to the Native Instruments YouTube channel for a host of Tracktor DJ tutorials: www.youtube.com/user/NativeInstruments/videos?sort=dd&tag_id=UCwjiBFz7LuxYvmIRw5kChFA.3.traktor&shelf_id=2&view=46.

> **Tip:** There are several ways to access your music library. You can save tracks directly to your iPad by transferring them with iTunes, including saving songs to your iPad and using cloud-based options such as iCloud (see chapter 1). Most of the DJ apps cannot access DRM-protected tracks or tracks that were purchased when iTunes used DRM encryption. They can be converted using iTunes Match: www.apple.com/itunes/itunes-match/.

Cross DJ HD by MIXVIBES ($7.99)
https://itunes.apple.com/us/app/cross-dj-hd-mix-your-music/id509520532?mt=8

Cross DJ requires iPad 2 or later (iOS5). It includes an impressive list of features, including mixing iTunes tracks in perfect sync, adding effects, loops and more. Record your set and share it on SoundCloud. Cross DJ uses the same engine as Pioneer's rekordbox.

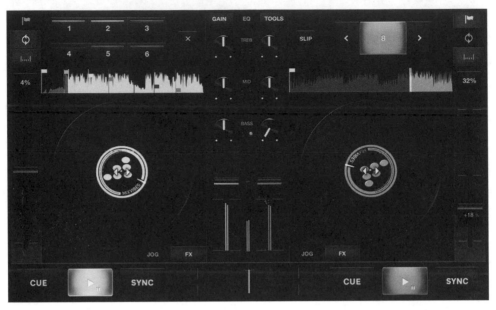

Figure 4.5 Cross DJ.

VIDEO 4.3 CROSS DJ DEMO.

Figure 4.6
http://youtu.be/4yNGqxi8CyE

DJ Rig for iPad By IK Multimedia ($19.99)
https://itunes.apple.com/us/app/id556542378?mt=8

DJ Rig's interface replicates a dual-deck hardware setup. Each deck routes to the iPad output jack (split stereo) so it can be used with the monitoring Y-cables mentioned later in this chapter. Each deck also has three visual modes: Vinyl, with tradition scratch effects; Digital, for CD jog wheel–style control; and Waveform, which includes cue points and syncing. DJ Rig includes an AutoMix feature that can cross-fade and mix music on its own, as well as other digital mixing aids that help align the beats of two tracks, such as Beat Match, Tempo Sync, and X-Sync.

DJ Rig serves up 18 tempo-synced effects: Delay, Flanger, Crush, HP filter, LP filter, BP filter, Compressor, Wah, Phaser, Fuzz, Reverb, and Stutter, plus 6 that IK claims are new for this release: Noise, Tail, Brake, Spin, Twist Up, and Twist Down.

Figure 4.7 DJ Rig.

VIDEO 4.4. DJ RIG DEMO.

Figure 4.8
http://youtu.be/VW-jsHYbSe4

Tip: If you want to have some fun with remixing, and you are new to the DJ world, Crossfader by DJZ is an excellent place to start. It requires iOS7 or later. The app is free and allows you to discover, remix, and share brilliant mashups, no experience required: https://itunes.apple.com/us/app/crossfader/id628517073?mt=8.

Monitoring with Y-Cables

When you are using just your iPad as your DJ unit, you will need a way to monitor for cueing. You can accomplish this with a cable that connects to the audio output of the iPad. Plug your headphones into the headphone jack and the output to your speakers from the other jack. Then choose the appropriate settings in the app so you can monitor the tracks you want to bring up next.

Traktor DJ Cable ($9.99)

www.native-instruments.com/en/products/traktor/traktor-for-ios/traktor-dj-cable/

The cable is made with silver-plated, oxygen-free copper on the inside and gold-plated mini jack connectors at the ends for optimum audio clarity. Designed by the creators of Traktor DJ, it provides a solid base for connectivity with any sound system. It is designed for integration with Traktor DJ and also works well with your other favorite DJ apps and software.

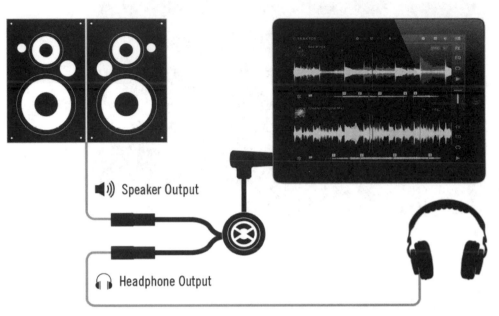

Figure 4.9 Traktor DJ Cable.

VIDEO 4.5 TRAKTOR DJ CABLE DEMO.

Figure 4.10
http://youtu.be/fwONtshTCbE

DJ Cable by Griffin ($19.99)

http://store.griffintechnology.com/dj-cable

Made for the djay app by Algoriddim, DJ Cable lets you cue up your next track and hear what's playing at the same time. Your DJ Cable is wired to enable djay's Split Output function, so you can cue up independently of the speaker mix.

The DJ Cable has gold connectors for improved conductivity (and thus a better signal), as well as a braided exterior for durability. With Split Output mode enabled, djay sends the master output to the left channel and the cue output to the right channel. This lets you cue songs through your headphones independently of the mix that's going through the speakers. At the same time, you can hear everything that's going on. No DJ would want to be without it!

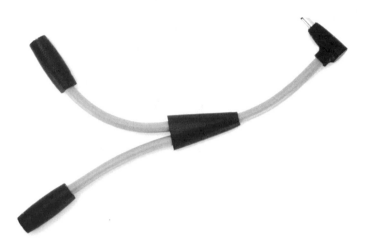

Figure 4.11. DJ Cable by Griffin.

> **Tip:** A great way to listen to and post DJ content and mixes is by using Mixcloud: http://support.mixcloud.com/. It is designed for everyone who enjoys listening to radio and DJ content and for DJs who are looking for better ways to host and promote their mixes and cloudcasts online. Mixcloud—Radio & DJ Mixes by Mixcloud (free) https://itunes.apple.com/us/app/mixcloud-radio-dj-mixes/id401206431?mt=8

DJ Mixers

There are two categories of DJ hardware mixers:
- Those designed to be directly connected to the iPad.
- Those that can be connected to the iPad via the Apple Camera Connection Kit.

This section focuses on hardware designed to be directly connected to the iPad via the 30-pin or Lightning connector. With these devices, you will be able to attach headphones for monitoring, and since the device also includes physical platters, you can use them to create your mixes and for live performance.

iRig Mix ($99.99)
www.ikmultimedia.com/products/irigmix/

Specifically designed to connect to the iPad, the iRig Mix can just be plugged into the 30-pin or Lightning connector, and you are ready to go. You can mix and crossfade between two stereo tracks, lining up tracks with the built-in Cue system while your mix plays out of the main outputs. You get a two-band EQ for each input, and you can also connect a microphone for mixing in vocals. There's also an instrument input for connecting an electric guitar, bass, or electronic keyboard. And the unit is light and very portable.

The iRig Mix comes with IK Multimedia's iRig DJ app mentioned earlier in this chapter, and it's also compatible with many other DJ apps available for the iPad.

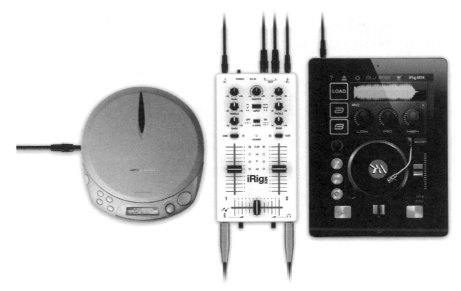

Figure 4.12 iRig Mix with iPad and CD Player.

VIDEO 4.6 IRIG MIX DEMO.

Figure 4.13
http://youtu.be/FcJfBmSmIQY

Tip: When you have a separate mixer, you can use two iPads to give you more control over your setup. Check out this video using two iPads with an iRig Mix.

VIDEO 4.7 IRIG MIX WITH 2 IPADS DEMO.

Figure 4.14
http://youtu.be/SWOKRYVw_70

DJ Connect by Griffin ($99)

http://store.griffintechnology.com/dj-connect

DJ Connect, made for Algoriddim's djay app (mentioned previously in this chapter), allows you to pre-cue your music and beat mix, with the added benefits of volume control, dual separate stereo outputs, and three detachable cables. It can be used with iPads with the Apple 30-pin dock connectors or Lightning connectors with the 30-pin to Lightning connector (see chapter 1). Plug your headphones into the yellow headphone port in the front, and connect your external speakers to the RCA line level stereo outputs on the back. A yellow glow underneath will illuminate to provide ambient light when spinning in the dark. The unit is compact: approximately 3 inches long, 2 inches wide, and 1.5 inches deep.

Figure 4.15 Griffin DJ Connect.

VIDEO 4.8 DJ CONNECT DEMO.

Figure 4.16
http://youtu.be/UNKo4pKatUo

Traktor Kontrol Z1 by Native Instruments ($199)

www.native-instruments.com/en/products/traktor/traktor-for-ios/traktor-kontrol-z1/

Traktor Kontrol Z1 is the ultracompact 2-channel mixer, controller, and soundcard for Traktor DJ and Traktor Pro 2. It features:
- Complete, ultraportable setup for Traktor DJ.
- Pro-quality knobs, faders, and backlit buttons.
- Mixing interface with three-band EQ; built-in 24-bit soundcard.

Native Instruments' Traktor Kontrol Z1 mixer module brings powerful hands-on mixing control to your digital DJ rig. Designed to integrate effortlessly with Traktor DJ (for iOS) and Traktor Pro 2, the Traktor Kontrol Z1 is both the intuitive controller you've been looking for and the high-end 24-bit/96 kHz audio interface your music deserves. All three of its faders are extremely touch responsive, and you'll be blown away by the feel and texture of each knob. And to top it off, there's even a full cue controller onboard the Native Instruments Traktor Kontrol Z1.

Figure 4.17. Traktor Kontrol Z1.

VIDEO 4.9 TRAKTOR KONTROL Z1 DEMO.

Figure 4.18
http://youtu.be/QXaD3KZ_2T0

DJ Mixers with Platters

The next options up is to use a DJ mixer that also includes physical platters. This gives you the alternative to use either the iPad app or the hardware platters for mixing.

iDJ Live II by Numark ($99.99 list price)
www.numark.com/product/idj-live-ii

iDJ Live is designed to integrate with Traktor DJ, mentioned above. It can be connected directly to the iPad via either a 30-pin or Lightning connector. It is both a controller and a 24-bit/96 kHz audio interface. The iDJ Live gives you hands-on mixing control. All three of its faders are touch responsive, and it features a full cue controller onboard. It includes two large performance turntables and a central mixer section with a cross-fader. Just load your tracks to either Deck 1 or Deck 2, and then control it, cueing up the start point, performing advanced transitions, and if you want, scratching. It can also be connected via USB to a Mac or Windows computer.

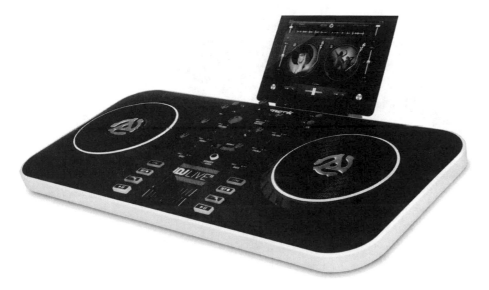

Figure 4.19 iDJ Live II.

VIDEO 4.10 IDJ LIVE II DEMO.

Figure 4.20
http://youtu.be/sUXFhycSOgs

DJ DDJ-WeGO2 by Pioneer ($249 list price)
http://www.pioneerelectronics.com/PUSA/DJ/Controllers/DDJ-WeGO2

The DDJ-WeGO2 is a compact DJ controller. Much like its predecessor, the DDJ-WeGO2 offers advanced functions, and features include Jog FX, Pulse Control, and multicolor LED illumination. The DDJ-WeGO2 is available in white, black, and red to complement the user's preference taste and color, and matched to the popular HDJ-500 DJ headphones. Designed for DJ software such as Algoriddim Inc.'s djay (mentioned previously in this chapter), the controller also features multicolor LED backlighting for the Jog wheel and a customizable (color) user interface for the included software.

Figure 4.21 DJ DDJ-WeGO2.

VIDEO 4.11 DJ DDJ-WEGO2 DEMO.

Figure 4.22
http://youtu.be/rG32ZeKkB6E

Traktor Kontrol S4 MK2 by Native Instruments ($899 list price)

http://www.native-instruments.com/en/products/traktor/dj-controllers/traktor-kontrol-s4/

The Traktor Kontrol S4 combines a premium 4-channel mixer, a built-in 24-bit/96 kHz soundcard, and an intuitive interface, and integrates with Native Instruments' Traktor DJ app reviewed previously in this chapter. It is an ideal one-stop package for DJs who want pro features, instant usability, and go-anywhere portability. It provides you with a DJ rig that performs like standalone hardware but offers the extreme flexibility of software. Juggle beats, fire off loops, add effects, and scratch the Traktor DJ app.

Figure 4.23 Traktor Kontrol S4 MK2.

VIDEO 4.12 TRAKTOR KONTROL S4 DEMO.

Figure 4.24
http://youtu.be/3ZYiOV9g6aA

Mixdeck Quad by Numark ($999 list price)
www.numark.com/product/mixdeckquad

Numark's Mixdeck Quad is a complete DJ system with an integrated four-channel mixer. Based upon Numark's popular Mixdeck controller, Mixdeck Quad supports apps such as Algoriddum's djay, mentioned previously in this chapter. There's also a fully functional four-channel digital/analog MIDI mixer, letting you control both the iPad and DJ software while mixing from CDs, thumb drives, mics, or external sources. Features include Tap Tempo and BPM (beats per minute) analysis. Enhance your performances with the integrated beat-synced DSP effects available on each one of Mixdeck Quad's decks, including echo, filter, flanger, pan, and phaser—each completely tweakable. A dedicated fader gives you control over the wet-dry mix.

Figure 4.25 Mixdeck Quad.

VIDEO 4.13. MIXDECK QUAD DEMO.

Figure 4.26
http://youtu.be/sBHZYgIwXgY

Controlling External Devices via the Apple Camera Connection Kit

All of the devices in this chapter were designed for connecting to an iPad via the 30-pin or Lightning connector. In addition to purchasing an iPad-ready device, you can use other devices that are class compliant (see chapter 1). If you own or have access to a USB device that is class compliant, you can connect it to your iPad via the Apple Camera Connection Kit (see chapter 1). Examples include the Numark DJ 2 Go (www.numark.com/product/dj2go) and audio interfaces such as the Alesis io2Express: www.alesis.com/io2express.

As mentioned in chapter 1, some devices that are not class compliant can still be used by plugging them into a USB hub to supply the necessary power to the device. Of course it is easier to purchase one of the iPad class compliant devices that are reviewed in this and other chapters. However, if you do have access to class compliant USB devices, you may be able to use them by plugging them into the Apple Camera Connection Kit. It is important to follow a specific procedure when connecting class compliant USB devices to your iPad.

1. Connect the USB cable to your Audio or MIDI device.
2. Connect the other end of the USB cable to the iPad Camera Connection Kit adapter (see chapter 1).
3. Connect the Camera Connection Kit adapter (with the USB cable already attached) to the 30-pin or Lightning port on the iPad.
4. Wait approximately 10 seconds. The iPad will take a few moments to fully recognize a connected device.

If the class compliant device does not function within 10 seconds after connecting it to your iPad, the device likely requires more power than the iPad can supply. The next option is to try connecting the device to a powered USB hub.

VIDEO 4.14. CONNECTING A CLASS COMPLIANT USB DEVICE.

Figure 4.27
http://vimeo.com/87752576

Headphones

You will need a quality set of headphones to monitor your mixes. Although any stereo headphone can be used, there are some that are specifically designed for DJs. Basically, you want to use a headphone that allows you to hear what you are mixing.

Behringer HPX2000 Headphones ($19.95)
www.behringer.com/EN/Products/HPX2000.aspx

These are closed, circumaural headphones designed for DJ use. They deliver a wide frequency response and high dynamic range.

Figure 4.28. Behringer HPX2000 Headphones.

Sennheiser HD 201 Headphones ($29.95 list price)
http://en-us.sennheiser.com/over-ear-headphones-hd-201

These lightweight, supra-aural headphones provide dynamic audio with crisp bass and good external noise attenuation without breaking the bank, and are excellent for DJ work.

Figure 4.29. Sennheiser HD 201 headphones.

HDJ-1000 Headphones by Pioneer ($179 list price)
www.pioneerelectronics.com/PUSA/DJ/Headphones/HDJ-1000+Limited

The HDJ-1000 headphones provide the high-quality sound as well as choices of colors and styles that make a fashion statement. The HDJ-1000 headphones come in two new colors: black and gold. To obtain the best audio reproduction possible, the drivers in the HDJ-1000 headphones were tuned to deliver more impact in the lower bass frequencies of music. Their thick 38-micrometer diaphragm and 1.5 millimeter voice coil are more efficient than other headphones in generating the critical midrange and mid-bass frequencies in music, and they produce a more linear response, even at high volume levels.

The mono/stereo selector circuit was modified to obtain clearer playback, especially in the midrange frequencies. With this change, the headphones deliver sounds such as bass drums, snare drums, and cymbals with more impact.

For maximum comfort, the headphones use low rebound urethane for the ear pads, providing a better fit and increased comfort when used for long DJ sessions. Along with the urethane pads, the design of the headphones, wrapping around the ears to achieve excellent sound insulation, makes monitoring effortless, even in the noisiest environments.

Additional features of the HDJ-1000 include an easy fold-away structure design, a convenient carrying pouch, a swivel mechanism with 90-degree housing rotation to support a wide range of monitoring styles, and a convenient mono/stereo switch for single-ear use.

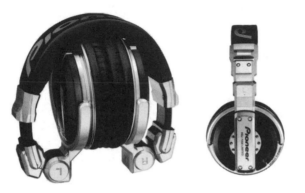

Figure 4.30 HDJ-1000 Headphones.

iPad Stands

Stands for the iPad were introduced in chapter 2. Many of these can be used to enhance a DJ setup such as the IK Multimedia iKlip Stand iPad: http://www.ikmultimedia.com /products/iklipstand/.

Figure 4.31. IK Multimedia iKlip Stand iPad.

Amplification

You can use any speakers for your DJ needs either by via a Y-jack and sending the output to your speakers or amplifier, or connecting the output of your DJ mixer to the sound. Going through a complete review of speakers for DJ needs is beyond the scope of this chapter and book. This section will focus on all-in-one systems for the iPad and wireless speakers.

All-in-One Systems for the iPad

There are a growing number of all-in-one systems that are designed for use with the iPad. The advantage is that all components—the power amp, platters, and speakers—are built in, making it compact and easy to transport.

Philips M1X-DJ Sound System for iPad ($399.95)

www.ifa.philips.com/

M1X-DJ combines a DJ mixer/platter and sound system in one compact box. It comes with a Lightning connector for connecting an iPad. It has Bluetooth connectivity and works seamlessly with the djay 2 app from Algoriddim mentioned previously in this chapter.

Using the djay 2 app, you can switch between tracks on your playlist or mix tracks as you choose. The integrated DJ controller allows you to mix and scratch your music using two professional grade platters, cross faders, and controls. The MIX-DJ is on the pricey side, at 399.95 Euros, or approximately 542.64 United States dollars.

Figure 4.32. Philips M1X-DJ Sound System.

Wireless Powered Speakers

Another option is to go with powered speakers that are Bluetooth ready so the iPad can connect to them wirelessly.

Ion Audio Tailgater Portable AM/FM Speaker with Bluetooth ($249.99)

www.ionaudio.com/products/details/tailgaterbluetooth

Ion's Tailgater Bluetooth is a portable sound system that includes speakers, an amplifier, audio inputs, and wireless Bluetooth technology, all in one durable cabinet that has handles for easy transport. Tailgater Bluetooth has a built-in battery with a charge indicator and will provide up to 50 hours of cordless sound. Or you can use the included power cord and rock out as long as you want. A built-in USB 2.0 port provides charging for the iPad or other iOS devices. The unit includes a microphone and the ability to amplify your guitar, keyboard, CD player, or other audio sources.

Figure 4.33. Ion Audio Tailgater.

Behringer Europort MPA40BT-Pro ($299.99 list price)
www.behringer.com/EN/Products/MPA40BT-PRO.aspx

The Behringer Europort MPA40BT-Pro is an all-in-one portable Bluetooth-enabled PA system designed for live-sound reinforcement applications. The speaker can be powered by an AC power cord or by the built-in rechargeable battery with a run time of up to 12 hours. The unit features an 8-inch full-range woofer that is powered by 40 watts of amplification. A built-in 2.4 GHz Bluetooth receiver allows you to stream music to the PA system from smartphones, tablets, computers, and other Bluetooth-enabled devices. You can also connect up to two Behringer ULM wireless microphones using the PA system's USB wireless port and a compatible ULM USB wireless microphone receiver key (sold separately).

For wired connections, the unit features two XLR microphone inputs (see chapter 5) with independent level controls. The system comes with one wired dynamic microphone and microphone cable. The PA also features an aux RCA input pair with independent level control for connecting to a line level source such as a CD player. The output control for the unit features bass and treble controls as well as a knob for adjusting the master output level. A built-in 35-millimeter socket on the bottom of the speaker enables mounting the unit on a stand. For portability, the pro version of the PA system features built-in rolling wheels and an extendable handle.

Figure 4.34. Behringer Europort MPA40BT-Pro.

Samson Exhibition Express (list price: $279.99 for one speaker)
www.samsontech.com/samson/products/portable-pa/expedition/expeditionexpress/

Samson's Expedition Express is an all-in-one PA system that lets you take your music wherever you need to go. It includes Bluetooth technology to connect wireless with your iPad. It has a three-channel mixer and a two-band EQ, so setting it up with your iPad will take no time at all. It also has an eight-hour rechargeable battery, so you can go wireless and plug into AC if available. With its ultralightweight design and integrated carrying handles, it is an excellent choice for powered Bluetooth speakers for your DJ rig.

Figure 4.35. Samson Exhibition Express.

Interview with DJ Paul Geissinger

In chapter 8, we focus on using the iPad with computers and mixers. There are also many options for using the iPad in a DJ setup in a similar manner. This interview will focus on using the iPad with computer-based software.

VIDEO 4.15. INTERVIEW WITH DJ PAUL GEISSINGER: "THE IPAD IN THE COMPUTER-BASED DJ SET-UP."

Figure 4.36
http://vimeo.com/87750759

DJ Gear Options

The following are four sample low-, moderate-, and high-cost options for DJ gear. These are designed to serve as a starting-off point. Customize this for your personal use.

DJ Gear Option 1 (low to moderate cost)

One iPad and a DJ app, IK stand, Griffin monitor cable, and headphones; use AirPlay to send the output to a wireless Bluetooth speaker, or use the iPad all-in-one.

- iPad: starting at $499.00
- DJ app: $4.99–$19.99
- iPad stand: $19.99–$69.00
- Y-cable for monitoring: $9.99–$19.99
- headphones: $19.95
- Bluetooth speaker: $279.99

Total cost: $833.91–$907.92

DJ Gear Option 2 (moderate cost)

One iPad and a DJ app, IK stand, DJ mixer without platters, headphones, and Bluetooth speaker.

- iPad: starting at $499.00
- DJ app: $4.99–$19.99
- iPad stand: $19.99–$69.00
- DJ hardware mixer: $99.00–$199.00
- headphones: $29.95
- Bluetooth speaker: $279.99–$299.99

Total cost: $932.92–$1,116.93

DJ Gear Option 3 (moderate to high cost)

iPads and DJ app, IK stand, mixer with platters, headphones, and speaker.

- iPad: starting at $499.00
- DJ app: $4.99–$19.99

- iPad stand: $19.99–$69.00
- DJ hardware mixer with platters: $99.00–$999.00
- headphones: $29.95
- Bluetooth speaker: $279.99–$299.99

Total cost: $932.92–$1,916.93

DJ Gear Option 4 (high cost)

Two iPads and DJ app, IK stand, mixer with platters;, headphones, and speaker.

- 2 iPads: starting at $499.00–$998.00
- DJ app: $4.99–$19.99
- iPad stand: $19.99–$69.00
- DJ hardware mixer with platters: $99.00–$999.00
- headphones: $29.95–$179.00
- Bluetooth speaker: $279.99–$299.99

Total cost: $1,431.92–$2,564.98

Chapter 4 Activities

1. Download the free Crossfader app
   (https://itunes.apple.com/us/app/crossfader/id628517073?mt=8)
   and create a set list with fades.
2. Download the free app djay LE, and use it to create a set list and custom mixes.
3. Review the mixers and mixers with platters, and choose the one that best suits your needs and budget.
4. Try connecting a class compliant USB device to your iPad using the Apple Camera Connection Kit.
5. Connect the iPad to a Bluetooth-enabled speaker for wireless playback.
6. Choose a pair of headphones designed for DJ use.
7. Select one of the DJ gear options and make adjustments to it to suit your needs.

Summary

This chapter focused on DJ apps and gear designed to be used with the iPad. DJ apps were included with no equipment other than speakers for playback. The next option is to purchase a mixer, so you can connect two iPads or an iPad and CD player, microphone, instrument, or other electronic device. DJ mixers that also include two hardware platters were also introduced. All-in-one iPad speakers were included, along with iPad stands and sample DJ gear options.

Chapter 5

EXTERNAL MICS AND MONO/STEREO RECORDING

This chapter focuses on connecting microphones to your iPad for use with audio and video recording apps. There is a built-in microphone in the iPad; however, this chapter deals with connecting an external microphone to improve on the recording quality of the built-in mic. Also included is an overview of the common microphone types and pickup patterns. Since the iPad can be used as the main part of your audio studio (see chapters 6 and 7) and as a portable unit for "field" recording, there are a myriad of options to consider.

Microphone Basics

The purpose of a microphone is to convert a sound wave into an electrical impulse and pass it along the signal chain. That sounds like a very straightforward task; however, in the audio world it is as complex as an art form. Things to consider include the construction of the microphone and the placement of it in relation to the sound source, as well as the processing of the electrical impulse as it moves through the signal chain. The iPad's built-in mic does not capture the full dynamic range compared to external mics, and therefore, if quality recording is the goal, an additional external mic is needed.

There are a number of different types of microphones, which could be the topic of one or more books. This chapter is limited to commonly used microphones in audio production—specifically, dynamic, condenser, and ribbon microphones.

Dynamic Microphones

Dynamic microphones, or dynamic mics, are also called moving coil mics. They are the most durable in construction and can handle almost any sound pressure level. Dynamic mics respond best to percussive sounds but not so well for less intense sound pressure levels, such as those produced by a saxophone or violin. Dynamic microphones are most frequently used for live sound applications, including speeches, concerts, and TV news reporting.

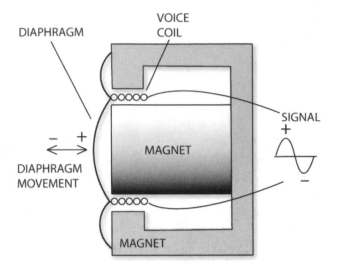

DIAPHRAGM

VOICE
COIL

DIAPHRAGM
MOVEMENT

− +

MAGNET

SIGNAL
+

−

MAGNET

Dynamic transducer

Figure 5.01. Dynamic microphone diagram.

Since the sound pressure from a snare drum is different than that from a saxophone, different microphones are typically used. Dynamic mics handle intense sound waves best, so they are suited to place near a snare drum or guitar amp. An example of a popular dynamic mic is the Shure SM57.

Figure 5.02. Shure SM57.

Tip: Not all dynamic mics are well suited for every recording situation. The sound pressure from a bass drum is similar to the intensity of the snare drum; however, the SM57 does not respond as well to lower frequencies, so a different type of dynamic mic is typically used in the studio, such as the AKG D112, one of the most popular bass drum mics.

Figure 5.03. AKG D112.

Condenser Microphones

Condenser mics are the most common in the recording studio. A good condenser mic can work well for most acoustic instruments and vocals. Condenser mics do not respond well to loud, intense sounds. They are so sensitive that overly strong sound pressure signals can damage them. The diaphragm is the vibrating part of the condenser microphone's pickup.

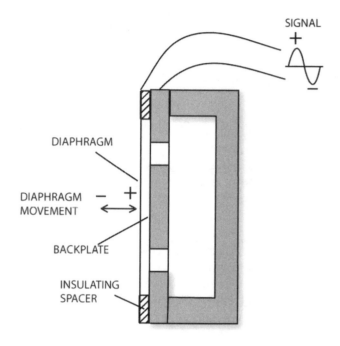

Condenser Transducer

Figure 5.04. Condenser mic diagram.

Condenser mics are available in two sizes: large diaphragm and small diaphragm. The large diaphragm mic is more sensitive and has a narrower frequency range than the small diaphragm. By comparison, a small diaphragm mic can handle higher-pressure sound waves and has a wider frequency range.

The Microtech Geffel UMT70S (see Figure 5.05) is a large diaphragm mic, and it is the microphone I use the most in my studio. I use it for vocals and solo acoustic instruments. The Earthworks TC 30K (see figure 5.06) is a small diaphragm condenser mic, and I use this for recording large ensembles such as choirs and orchestras, in both the studio and live settings.

Figure 5.05. Microtech Geffel UMT70S.

Figure 5.06. Earthworks TC 30K small diaphragm microphone.

Condenser microphones require 48 volts of power to operate, referred to as *phantom power*. Phantom power can be provided to the condenser mic via a built-in battery or by connecting it to a phantom power capable audio mixer (see chapter 8).

> **Tip:** Before plugging a condenser microphone into a phantom power–capable mixer or iPad audio interface (see chapter 6), be sure phantom power is turned off. Turn phantom power on after the mic is connected, and turn it off before unplugging the mic from the mixer or interface.

There are many makes and models of condenser microphones on the market at a wide range of price points. A comprehensive evaluation is beyond the scope of this book. Consult with your local music dealer, and be sure to listen to the mic before purchasing.

Ribbon Microphones

Ribbon microphones were the endangered species of the microphone world for a time, but they have enjoyed a little resurgence today. As recording technology leapt into the digital age, very little has changed in the microphone world. Ribbon mics are the most fragile of the three types, and RCA, manufacturer of the classic models, stopped making them in 1954. Those lucky enough to own them found it difficult to keep them in repair. But the mellow sound of old gear like ribbon mics turned out to be just the thing digital recordings needed to provide much-needed warmth. Today's ribbon mics are more durable but a little more expensive than most condenser models. A ribbon mic is a great addition to any microphone collection, but I would not recommend it as the first one to purchase.

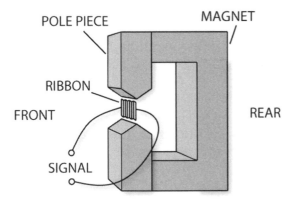

Ribbon Transducer

Figure 5.07. Ribbon microphone diagram.

Shock Mount

The Blue Microphones Woodpecker Ribbon Microphone (see figure 5.08) is mounted in a shock mount. The shock mount isolates it from any vibration coming from the mic stand.

Figure 5.08. Blue Microphones Woodpecker Ribbon Microphone with shock mount.

Microphone Pickup Patterns

Every microphone has a pickup pattern, or area around the microphone capsule where it "hears" best.

Omnidirectional

Omnidirectional pattern mics, or omnis, pick up sound equally in all directions. This is ideal when you need to record everything going on around you without constantly pointing or re-aiming the mic. Omnis are popular with TV news field reporters and for recording meetings.

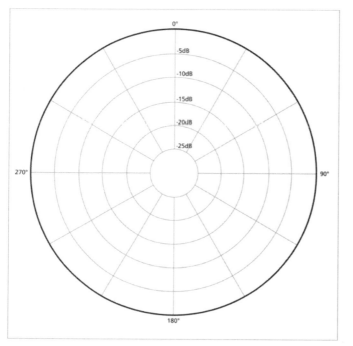

Figure 5.09. Omnidirectional pickup pattern.

Bidirectional

A bidirectional pattern uses both sides of a microphone diaphragm to record in a "figure 8" pattern. Both sides of the capsule are used to record a single track. This pattern is most used in the mid-side recording technique, where the bidirectional mic is used to record the "side" track. In this technique, two microphones, one using a cardioid pattern and one using a bidirectional pattern, record two mono tracks. The side track audio file is duplicated on a second track in a DAW program (so there are now three tracks, including the mid-track), and then the second side track's polarity is reversed, throwing it out of phase with the original track. One of the side tracks is panned hard left and the other hard right. The mid track by itself will sound like a mono recording, but when the two side tracks are played with the mid track, the stereo field can be heard. The width of the stereo field is determined by the volume of the side tracks; louder volume produces a wider stereo image.

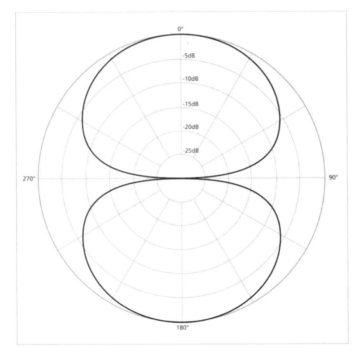

Figure 5.10. Bidirectional pickup pattern.

Cardioid

When recording a specific source, a unidirectional mic is best, because it is sensitive to sounds only in one direction. The most common unidirectional microphone is a cardioid microphone, which has a pickup pattern shaped like a human heart (see Figure 5.11). A cardioid mic pointed at the stage in a live setting will record less of the audience room sound located behind the mic.

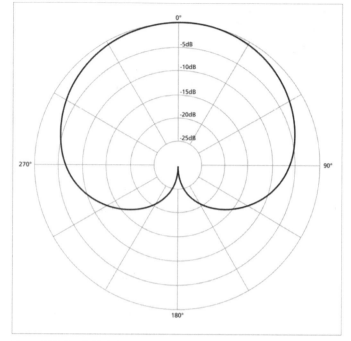

Figure 5.11. Cardioid pickup pattern.

There are variations of the cardioid pattern that have a narrower pickup field and can record at a greater distance from the sound source. A popular option is the shotgun mic (see Figure 5.12). A shotgun mic can record up to 3 feet away. It is used primarily in video production, where the mic must record a narrow portion of the audio spectrum. The longer the microphone tube, the more directional the pickup pattern.

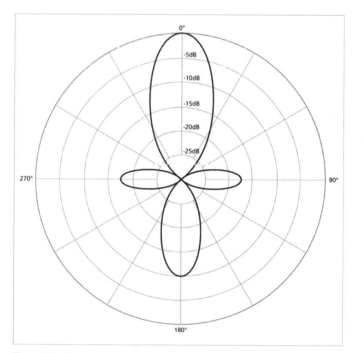

Figure 5.12. Shotgun pickup pattern.

External Microphones Designed for the iPad

The microphones listed in this chapter fall in into the dynamic and condenser categories, as ribbon mics are too fragile to use in the field or on location. And all of the mics connect directly to the iPad, so they are easy to use. These external mics are designed for recording spoken word and audio for video, rehearsals, and live performance. If you are interested in connecting mics to external audio interfaces, see chapter 6.

Field Recording

Field recording is the term used for an audio recording produced outside of a recording studio, or "in the field." This also includes using the iPad to record practice sessions and make reference recordings of live performances. Field recording mics connect directly to the iPad and are suitable for rehearsal and concert recordings, sound effects recording, and podcasting.

iPads are ideal for field recording, as they are light and portable and make no noise during operation. Computers have fans that can create unwanted noise. When recording with the iPad, be sure to use the iPad Settings app and switch to Airplane mode (see chapter 1). This will prevent interruptions from e-mail or text message alerts.

> **Tip:** Stereo mics have two capsules arranged in a preset pickup pattern. This takes the place of using two separate microphones to create a stereo recording. Make sure the app you are using supports stereo recording before attempting it in the field.

Figure 5.13. TASCAM iM2X.

iRig Mic Cast by IK Multimedia ($39.99)
www.ikmultimedia.com/products/irigmiccast/

The iRig Mic Cast provides an excellent alternative to the iPad's internal mic when recording to an audio app (see chapter 7). It can also be used for video recording. The mic has a switch on the front to adjust for close or distance recording. It connects to the iPad headphone jack and is designed to create a secure connection even when the iPad is in a case. There is a headphone jack on the side of the mic so you can monitor sound while recording. The iRic Mic Cast also works with the iPhone, and it comes with a stand to position the iPhone for better recording. To position the iPad for recording, use one of the iPad cases mentioned in chapter 1.

Figure 5.14. iRig Mic Cast.

VIDEO 5.1. IRIG MIC CAST DEMO.

Figure 5.15.
http://youtu.be/DIIkwVZL1dw

iM2 by TASCAM ($99.99 list price)
http://tascam.com/product/im2/

The TASCAM iM2 includes two cardioid pattern condenser microphone small diaphragms and mounts them together in an A-B pattern or spaced pair to create a stereo microphone.

The A and B mic capsules are pointed in opposite directions to cover large sound sources, including bands and orchestras of all sizes. The capsules can be manually rotated for aiming at the source.

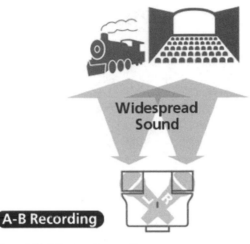

Figure 5.16. A-B microphone pattern.

The iM2 can handle higher decibel levels than the iPad's built-in mic (a decibel is a unit of measurement used to describe the power or loudness of sound), and the A/D converters deliver CD-quality sound.

The iM2 is designed for live and rehearsal recording, recording sound effects, and replacing the iPad's internal mic for video recording. It has a control wheel for input volume and a USB connector for charging the iPad while recording. You can also purchase the WS-2i windscreen ($14.99) to minimize wind noise.

Figure 5.17. TASCAM iM2.

VIDEO 5.2. TASCAM IM2 DEMO.

Figure 5.18.
http://youtu.be/5APO9aLzgtw

iM2X by TASCAM ($99.99 list price)

http://tascam.com/product/im2x/overview/

The iM2X microphone is identical to the iM2 but with the microphones configured in an X-Y stereo pattern. This X-Y pattern records a stereo image that is narrower and more focused than the A-B pattern of the iM2.

Figure 5.19. X-Y microphone pattern.

The iM2X is better suited for recording speeches, lectures, small ensemble music rehearsals or performances, sound effects, and audio for video. The microphone plugs into the 30-pin or Lightning connector of the iPad. An added feature of this mic is that the capsules can be manually rotated in order to be properly aimed toward the recording source.

Figure 5.20. TASCAM iM2X.

Mikey Digital by Blue Microphones ($99.99)

http://bluemic.com/mikey_digital/

The Mikey Digital is a stereo microphone with two cardioid condenser microphones mounted in a single housing, and it delivers CD-quality sound. The microphone housing rotates for precise aiming. A slide switch on the back of the mic sets its sensitivity to low, automatic, or high. LEDs on the front of the Mikey Digital indicate which sensitivity setting is currently selected; they also serve as peak indicators when the sound you are recording is too loud for the mic. There is a 1/8-inch jack line in on the top of the mic for connecting another audio source, such as the output of an MP3 player or electronic keyboard. It also includes a USB connector, making it possible to charge the iPad while recording. Mikey Digital's connector is 30-pin, but it can be connected to a Lightning port via the Apple Lightning to 30-pin adapter (see chapter 1).

Figure 5.21. Mikey Digital.

VIDEO 5.3. MIKEY DIGITAL DEMO.

Figure 5.22.
http://youtu.be/Xk7BJVXFNRo

iQ5 by ZOOM Corporation ($124.99 list price)
www.zoom.co.jp/products/iq5/features/

iQ5 comes with a Lightning connector and is only compatible with Lightning connector–equipped iPads. It has two condenser mics housed in a rotating ball for accurate aiming at the sound source. Aim the red dot on the mic housing at the audio source for best results.

iQ5 uses a mid-side recording technique to create a stereo field that is adjustable in width. In the mid-side technique, the "mid" microphone is set up facing the audio source, using a cardioid pickup pattern. This mic captures the direct sound of the source. The second or "side" microphone is positioned directly over, or under, with its capsule at a 90-degree angle to the mid mic. The side mic is set to a bidirectional or "figure 8" pattern and records room ambience.

Input volume is set by a control wheel on the side of the unit or by selecting Auto Gain on the front of the mic. For loud situations, a limiter can be switched on to minimize distortion. iQ5 also has a headphone jack, and a USB connector to allow the iPad to be charged while recording.

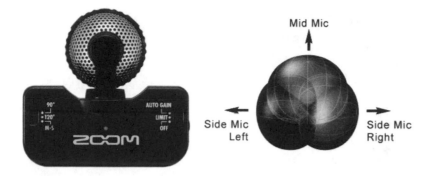

Figure 5.23. Zoom iQ5 and mid-side pickup pattern.

VIDEO 5.4. ZOOM IQ5 DEMO.

Figure 5.24.
http://youtu.be/sUDshiPvzW8

iXY by Røde ($299 list price)
www.rodemic.com/mics/ixy

iXY, as the name implies, is an X-Y pattern stereo microphone. The microphone capsules have cardioid pattern pickups and are housed in a sturdy metal enclosure. The mic is capable of delivering the highest-possible quality audio (96 kHz/24-bit) of any stereo microphone currently available for the iPad when using the RødeRec or RødeRec LE apps (mentioned in chapter 5 [page 95] of the *Musical iPad*).

Figure 5.25. Røde iXY.

VIDEO 5.4. RØDE IXY OVERVIEW

Figure 5.26.
http://youtu.be/Rqt1LouGAt8

MicW by iShotgun ($299 list price)
www.mic-w.com/product.php?id=77

MicW is a condenser mic with a hypercardioid pickup pattern, the standard for shotgun mics. Its purpose is for video and film recording where the mic must be out of the camera's view yet still able to record quality audio. Shotgun mics record midrange frequencies well, making them ideal for spoken word recording, but they are not as good for recording music. Due to the narrow focus of the pickup pattern, the mic must be precisely aimed. It is also very sensitive to handling noise when it is moved, so for live recording, it is best if it's mounted on a stand and not moved.

Figure 5.27. MicW.

VIDEO 5.5. MICW OVERVIEW.

Figure 5.28
http://youtu.be/c8tc9OXryk8

Podcasting and Spoken Word Recording

The microphones in this section are best suited for spoken word recording or for demos and reference recording. They require more care in handling than the field mics mentioned earlier, as handling noise will transfer to the recording. Touching or moving the mic, the mic stand, or the mic cable may produce audible noise in the recorded tracks.

iRig Mic by IK Multimedia ($59.99)

www.ikmultimedia.com/products/irigmic/

The iRig Mic is a condenser mic with a cardioid pickup pattern. It is designed for singers to use for practice and recording, and for live recording with an iPad. A slide switch on the microphone body changes the mic's sensitivity level from high to low as required by the specific recording situation. The mic's cable connects to the headphone jack of the iPad. The jack includes a 1/8-inch connector for headphones. A mic clip is included for mic stand mounting. The iRig Mic comes with the following apps:

- VocaLive Free (mentioned in chapter 5 [page 111] of the *Musical iPad*)
- AmpliTube Free (see chapter 3)
- iRig Recorder Free (introduced later in this chapter)

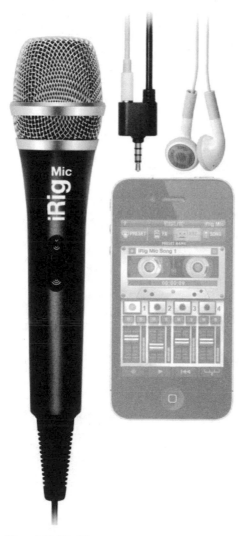

Figure 5.29. iRig Mic.

VIDEO 5.6. IRIG MIC OVERVIEW.

Figure 5.30
http://youtu.be/vvQBxDNIh6I

smartLav by Røde ($100 list price)
www.rodemic.com/mics/smartlav

Lavaliere mics physically clip onto a lapel or collar 6 to 8 inches from the speaker's mouth. The smartLav is a lavaliere condenser mic with an omnidirectional pickup pattern. Turning your head away from a cardioid mic results in a fast drop-off in vocal level. The omni pattern will keep the level constant even when the head moves while speaking. The smartLav plugs directly into the iPad's headphone jack. It works with the RødeRec and RødeRec LE apps, as well as any app that will accept input from the iPad's headphone jack, such as iRig Recorder.

Figure 5.31. smartLav microphone.

VIDEO 5.7. SMARTLAV RECORDING TIPS.

Figure 5.32
http://youtu.be/ymzEqVWc_ck

i436 Class 2 by MicW ($179)
www.mic-w.com/product.php?id=3

The i436 Class 2 is an omnidirectional condenser mic. It is designed to replace the iPad's microphone when working with acoustic analysis apps, covered later in this chapter. Its superior decibel range allows the app to make a more precise analysis. However, the i436 can be used for recording rehearsals or concerts and for podcasting. Since it is an omnidirectional mic, it is ideal for recording meetings or interviews. The mic's metal case doubles as a mic clip for stand mounting. It also comes with a small clip and extension cable for use as a lavaliere mic.

Figure 5.33. i436 microphone.

VIDEO 5.8. I436 MICROPHONE OVERVIEW.

Figure 5.34
http://youtu.be/CAFgx_IWJKw

Spark Digital by Blue Microphone ($199)
http://bluemic.com/spark_digital/

Spark Digital brings a microphone of professional recording studio quality to the iPad. It is a condenser microphone with a cardioid pickup pattern. Its stand is designed to eliminate table vibrations when mounted on a mic stand placed on a table. The microphone has its own headphone jack, so you can monitor its sound with zero latency from passing through the iPad. *Latency* refers to a short period of delay (usually measured in milliseconds) between when an audio signal enters and emerges from a system—in this case, the iPad and any apps processing the signal. There are controls for the input volume of the mic and the output volume for headphones. The Spark Digital is designed for spoken word, vocals, or live instruments.

The mic is available with both a 30-pin and Lightning iPad connector cable. To mount the Spark Digital on a microphone stand, you will need to purchase the Studio Accessory Bundle ($65) directly from the Blue Microphones service department. The bundle also includes a pop filter. The Spark can also connect to a computer via the included USB cable.

Figure 5.35. Spark Digital Microphone.

VIDEO 5.9. SPARK DIGITAL MICROPHONE OVERVIEW.

Figure 5.36.
http://youtu.be/Y1o921GHf40

MIC by Apogee ($199)
www.apogeedigital.com/products/mic.php

MIC by Apogee is a condenser microphone with a cardioid pickup pattern. The MIC is designed for versatile use, including spoken word, music, and audio for video. The MIC connects to the iPad via USB, which requires the Apple Camera Connector Kit (see chapter 1). It is designed primarily for use with multitrack recording apps, such as GarageBand and others mentioned in chapter 7. The MIC will also work with GarageBand on Mac computers. A microphone stand adapter is available for $19.95.

Figure 5.37. MIC by Apogee

MIC 96K by Apogee ($229)
www.apogeedigital.com/products/mic-96k.php

MIC 96K is an upgraded version of Apogee's MIC. The MIC 96K is capable of recording at 96 kHz/24-bit quality sound. Its operation and compatibility are the same as the MIC, mentioned above. Cables are included for iPads with 30-pin and Lightning connectors. The MIC 96K can also be connected to the iPad and Mac and PC computers via USB. It comes with a microphone stand adapter.

Figure 5.38. MIC 96K.

VIDEO 5.9A. MIC 96K DEMO.

Figure 5.39
http://youtu.be/SYZFWSRq-9c

> **Tip:** One way to keep your microphones sounding their best is by taking proper care of their cables. Careful handling and proper wrapping and storage will minimize damage. Damaged cables can create noise or dropouts during recording. To wrap the cables appropriately, gently loop the cable as you gather it up, and make sure it is not twisted. Secure it with a Velcro cable tie for storage.

iXJ2 Mic/Line Amplifier by TASCAM ($99.99 list price)
http://tascam.com/product/ixj2/

There are times when you will want to use a microphone for interviewing someone for a podcast or singing a solo with a mic while accompanying yourself with a guitar or electronic keyboard. The iXJ2 is designed for these applications, as it has two 1/8-inch connectors for separate mics or sound sources, or a combination of the two. There are two separate volume controls for each input and a built-in limiter to keep the audio from distorting. There is a USB connector for charging the iPad while you are recording. iXJ2 connects through the 30-pin port or the Apple 30-pin adapter to Lightning adapter. It works best with TASCAM's Linear PCM Recording app (introduced later in this chapter), but it also works with both versions of the RødeRec app.

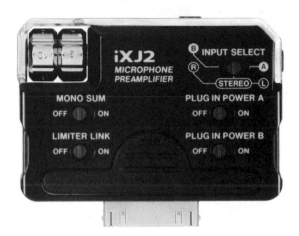

Figure 5.40. iXJ2 Mic/Line Amplifier.

Tip: The 30-pin to Lightning connector by Apple was introduced in chapter 1. You need to purchase this for any iPad mic or device that only supports the 30-pin connector. Be sure to check that the device will work with the 30-pin to Lightning connector, as not all devices are compatible with it.

Microphone Examples
In this video, you will hear a brief spoken word example, and an acoustic guitar sample recorded using some of the microphones listed in this chapter. The recording environment is a typical household space.

VIDEO 5.10. MICROPHONE EXAMPLES.

Figure 5.41
https://vimeo.com/87882407

Audio Recording Apps

For recording, you will need an app that records and stores the audio on your iPad. There are audio apps designed just for recording, and you can use multitrack apps such as those mentioned in chapter 7. The following section focuses on audio apps.

Mono and Stereo Recording Apps

The apps in this section record in both mono or stereo and are easy to use in the studio or in the field. Mono is a single channel of audio; stereo is either two channels recorded as a left-right pair or two separate sources isolated on individual tracks. The difference is the number of editing tools each app offers.

Tape by Focusrite by Novation (free)

https://itunes.apple.com/us/app/tape-by-focusrite/id681747796?mt=8

Tape by Focusrite is a free stereo or two-track recording app that is designed to accompany Focusrite's iTrack and Scarlett interfaces (see chapter 6). You can use the two tracks as a stereo pair or as individual inputs. Tape by Focusrite also supports all Core MIDI–compatible interfaces (see chapter 6), and it can be used with Audiobus (see chapter 7). There is a built-in metronome to keep your performances in sync, and you can monitor your recording through headphones. There are basic effects including reverb and EQ (equalization) that can be applied to recordings. After the recording is complete, it can be mastered using one of the presets. The resulting track can be uploaded to SoundCloud or exported via iTunes File Share.

Figure 5.42. Tape by Focusrite.

VIDEO 5.11. TAPE BY FOCUSRITE OVERVIEW.

Figure 5.43
http://youtu.be/sHfU-K0IMGM

Handy Recorder by ZOOM Corporation (free)
https://itunes.apple.com/us/app/handyrecorder/id566291779?mt=8

Handy Recorder can record in mono or stereo, using the iPad's built in mic or any microphone connected to the 30-pin or Lightning port of the iPad. You can record in WAV or AAC formats. Editing options include the ability to split a large file into smaller files. For example, you can record a concert and then split the recording into individual files by song. There are reverb and EQ effects as well as a mastering section where you can add compression and convert a stereo recording to mono if necessary.

Handy Recorder is designed to be used with the iQ5 microphone and work with its mid-side microphone configuration. Auto gain, direct monitoring, and left-right swap settings are only accessible with the iQ5 connected to the iPad. Handy Recorder does not share the iQ5's incompatibility with 30-pin iPads. Files can be uploaded to SoundCloud or transferred to a computer with iTunes File Share.

Figure 5.44. Handy Recorder.

iRig Recorder by IK Multimedia (free/in-app purchase)
https://itunes.apple.com/us/app/irig-recorder-free/id426702477?mt=8

The free version of iRig Recorder allows you to record audio and monitor the input recording level. It includes a Record button and can export your recording to SoundCloud, Wi-Fi, or FTP, or via iTunes File Sharing (see chapter 1).

In order to access the editing and effects features of iRig Recorder, you must purchase the full version via an in-app purchase of $7.99. The Optimize Level processor is included with the free version; the Processors Bundle, with seven other processors, is available as an in-app purchase for $4.99. The bundle includes the Cleanup processor, to remove background noise, and the Optimize Tone processor, which applies EQ. You can also use pitch shifting to move the key higher or lower or to change the speed of the recording without affecting pitch.

iRig Recorder supports the iRig microphone, as well as input from any 30-pin or Lightning source, such as the guitar interfaces mentioned in chapter 3 and the audio interfaces introduced in chapter 6. iRig Recorder also accepts input from other apps via Audiobus.

Figure 5.45. iRig Recorder.

VIDEO 5.12. IRIG RECORDER OVERVIEW.

Figure 5.46.
http://youtu.be/rBAoUPX67zA

PCM Recorder by TASCAM (free)
http://tascam.com/product/pcmrecorder/

PCM Recorder is a free app that is designed to work with TASCAM's iM2 and iM2X microphones and the iXJ2 mic preamp. The interface was originally designed for the iPhone, where the app fills the screen. The iPad version retains the iPhone screen layout in its original size and moves the app's buttons to the left side of the iPad screen. PCM Recorder can record in mono or stereo. Available effects include a limiter to minimize peaks in the recording, and high- and low-frequency EQ. You can transfer audio files to a Mac or PC computer via iTunes File Share and upload files to SoundCloud.

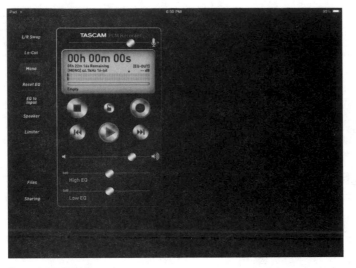

Figure 5.47. PCM Recorder.

Røde Rec by Røde Microphones ($5.99/LE version: free)
www.rodemic.com/software

Røde Rec, when combined with Røde's iXY microphone, offers high-resolution 48 kHz/24-bit recording in the free and paid versions of the app. The difference between the two versions is the ability to edit after recording. The LE is strictly a recorder with the options to share via SoundCloud, FTP, and iTunes File Share. The paid app has additional features for recording that include setting a countdown before the recording begins, recording for a specific amount of time, and recording until a specified time.

Computer software maker iZotope has provided some input processing effects to reduce unwanted high frequencies and low rumble. Editing on Røde Rec can be done in the iPad's landscape format so more of the waveform is visible. The app will automatically calculate how much recording time is possible at the chosen resolution. Both the free and paid versions can export files in a variety of audio formats, including WAV, AIFF, and AAC. The paid version can batch export files.

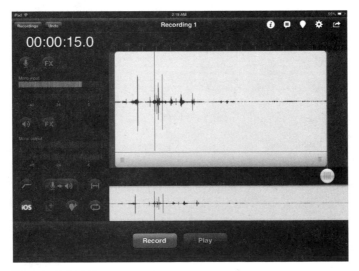

Figure 5.48. Røde Rec.

VIDEO 5.13. RØDE REC OVERVIEW.

Figure 5.49
http://youtu.be/i-mHx9gzYiA

TwistedWave Audio Editor by TwistedWave ($9.99)
https://itunes.apple.com/us/app/twistedwave-audio-editor/id401438496?mt=8

TwistedWave Audio Editor is a recorder with editing capabilities for both recordings you make and MP3 files from your iTunes library. You may record audio from other apps via Audiobus. There is a free app (TwistedWave Recorder; see the tip below) and a paid app (TwistedWave Audio Editor). The audio editor allows you to copy and paste audio, and undo or redo edits. In addition to copy and paste, you can send the entire audio file to other apps—for example, to create a loop. For users who want to create loops, the cut and paste option provides flexibility for working with different sound sources when exporting to another app.

TwistedWave includes effects for creating fade-ins and fade-outs, normalizing the volume level, pitch shifting, time stretching, compression, limiting, delay, and adding EQ. Audio files can be exported in WAV, AIFF, CAF, AAC, and MP3 file formats. Files can be exported via iTunes File Sharing, e-mail, or uploading to an FTP account or using cloud options such as Dropbox and SoundCloud. TwistedWave is also available for Mac computers.

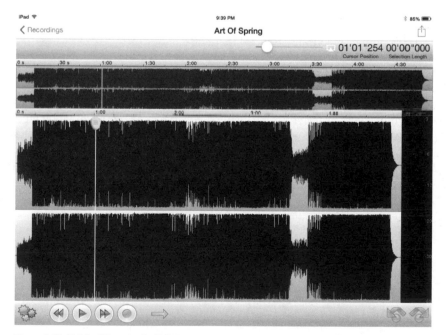

Figure 5.50. TwistedWave Audio Editor.

VIDEO 5.14. TWISTEDWAVE DEMO.

Figure 5.51.
http://youtu.be/C6URtEzxdvl

Tip: TwistedWave also offers a free lite version: "Twisted Wave Recorder." It has no editing features. https://itunes.apple.com/us/app/twistedwave-recorder/id690359266?mt=8

Audio Analysis

Audio is something professional engineers *listen* to, using practiced ears to judge the correct volume to balance each element of the mix. While the ear is always the final judge, audio analysis provides essential feedback about the audio signal, as well as the acoustic qualities of a studio space or concert hall. In any space, an engineer will want to know what frequencies may resonate naturally. If it is a concert hall, the engineer will take care not to boost any resonate frequencies, as the hall will amplify them. If feedback is a problem, analysis can locate the frequency range and lower it.

In a studio, acoustic treatments can be added to absorb sound in those frequencies. There are situations when an engineer's hearing may be compromised, due to illness, fatigue, air travel, drug effects, or deterioration due to aging. The visual feedback from an analysis app can be the tool that prevents overcorrection for tired ears.

RTA by Andrew Smith ($9.99)
https://itunes.apple.com/us/app/rta/id298839433?mt=8

RTA (Real Time Analysis) displays audio signals on a graph with the frequency divided into your choice of 1/3-octave or octave increments—from 20 Hz to 2000 Hz along the x-axis, and the full decibel range on the y-axis. Tapping the Play button along the bottom of the screen activates the display, which moves like a volume meter.

There is a tone generator that produces a variety of waves that play through the iPad's internal speaker or can be sent to a mixer via the headphone output. Wave options include sine, square, white noise, or pink noise. Pink noise is most commonly used to test signal, as it has equal energy in every octave.

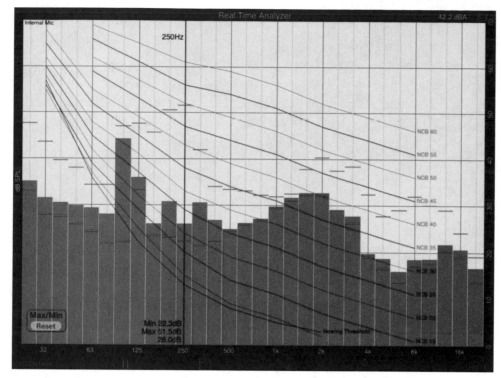

Figure 5.52. RTA.

VIDEO 5.15. RTA DEMO.

Figure 5.53
http://youtu.be/YfXsbpwnLZM

Spectrum Analyzer by ONYX Apps ($14.99)

https://itunes.apple.com/us/app/spectrum-analyzer/id490078884?mt=8

Spectrum Analyzer can perform real-time analysis as well as the more detailed Fast Fourier Transform, an algorithm that converts time or space to frequency. Real-time Analysis breaks the frequency spectrum into octave increments. A Fast Fourier Transform graphic display is shown in Figure 5.54. Spectrum Analyzer also has a Spectrograph display module and a Test Tone and White/Pink Noise generator.

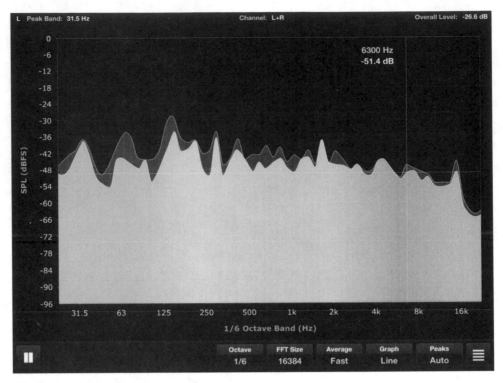

Figure 5.54. Spectrum Analyzer.

VIDEO 5.16. SPECTRUM ANALYZER DEMO.

Figure 5.55
http://youtu.be/DOwCKfRdn5k

PocketRTA HD—Spectrum Analyzer by 4Pockets.com ($39.99)
https://itunes.apple.com/us/app/pocketrta-hd-spectrum-analyzer/id378074484?mt=8

Pocket RTA HD provides fast and accurate spectrum analysis suitable for musicians and engineers. Pocket RTA HD samples sounds using either internal or external microphones, and then applies a Fast Fourier Transform to the samples to obtain a frequency spectrum. The result is an accurate representation of the sampled sound, broken down into its frequency components. You can use the iPad's multitouch screen to perform real-time magnification of displays. A noise cancellation system allows you to remove unwanted background noise.

Pocket RTA HD features the ability to calibrate the display using the 1/3, 1/6, or Octave display. The app can detect if an external microphone is being used, and switches to the correct calibration data for the mic. Pocket RTA HD has the ability to capture up to three input signals and overlay them as a reference as you continue to analyze a live signal in the app.

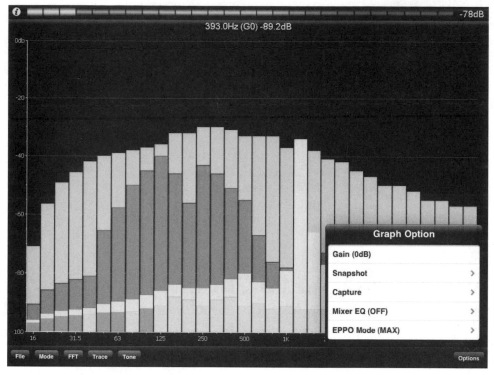

Figure 5.56. Pocket RTA HD.

VIDEO 5.17. POCKET RTA HD DEMO.

Figure 5.57
http://youtu.be/KsAC_3S7XFM

Tip: All audio analysis apps will provide much better results with an external microphone, such as the i436 mentioned earlier in this chapter. The i436 is created for analysis and connects directly with the iPad. Other analysis microphones, such as the Behringer ECM800, require phantom power and require an interface (see chapter 6) to work with the iPad.

Audio Analysis Interview with Andre Houser

VIDEO 5.18. POCKET RTA HD DEMO.

Figure 5.58
https://vimeo.com/87882511

Microphone Studio Options

One of the microphones listed in the chapter may suit your needs, or you may need to purchase a separate stereo mic and podcasting mic. Most engineers have microphone collections, not just one microphone, so you will likely purchase more than one over time. In the field microphone category, I recommend pairing a mic and app from the same company. For studio mics, the iRig Mic has several app choices, but the others are not associated with any software. For ease of editing, I'd recommend Røde Rec or TwistedWave, depending on your needs for processing and editing. In addition to the microphone, these units also function as A/D converters, so consider the resolution of the converters, as that will result in a higher-quality recording.

Field Recording Option 1 (low cost)
- iPad: starting at $499.00
- Microphone: $39.99
- Mono/stereo recording app: free–$7.99

Total cost: $539.00–$546.98

Studio Recording Option 1 (low cost)
- iPad: starting at $499.00
- Microphone: $59.99
- Mono/stereo recording and processing apps: free–$47.97

Total cost: $558.00–$606.96

Field Recording Option 2 (moderate cost)
- iPad: starting at $499.00
- Microphone: $99.99
- Mono/stereo recording app: free–$5.99
- Windscreen: $14.99

Total cost: $613.98–$619.97

Studio Recording Option 2 (lavaliere setup)
- iPad: starting at $499.00
- Microphone: $100.00–$200.00

- Mic/Lin Amplifier: $99.99
- Mono/stereo recording app: free–$5.99

Total cost: $698.99–$804.98

Field Recording Option 3 (high cost)

- iPad: starting at $499.00
- Microphone: $299.00
- Mono/stereo recording app: free–$5.99

Total cost: $798.00–$803.00

Studio Recording Option 3 (moderate–high cost)

- iPad: starting at $499.00
- Microphone: $199.00–$299.00
- Mono/stereo recording app: free–$9.99
- Microphone stand mount: $19.95–$199.99

Total cost: $717.95–$1,007.98

Activities

1. Turn on an audio source such as a TV or stereo system. Use one of the free recording apps, stand 2 feet in front of the audio source, and record 10 seconds of audio. Angle the mic off to the right or left and record 10 seconds more of audio. Back up a few feet and record 10 more seconds with the iPad's mic pointed directly at the sound source, and 10 seconds with the iPad's mic angled off to the side. If you have room, back up a few feet further and record another 10 seconds of direct audio and 10 of indirect audio. Compare the sound of the direct mic excerpts to the indirect. Then compare recordings at the different distances and note how the source interacts with the room. See if you can detect any frequency ranges that seem to ring in the room.

2. Try the same experiment in activity 1; however, this time, play your instrument or sing. Note the changes in sound as more room is introduced to the recording. Also listen for resonate frequencies in the room.

3. If you have a studio setup, try holding the iPad head-high at the spot where you listen. Try moving the iPad a foot forward, then a foot back from the spot. Then try a foot to the right and a foot to the left. Listen to the results, and see if you can detect differences in the music in each location.

Summary

In this chapter, we reviewed microphones suitable for recording vocals and instruments, spoken word, live concerts, rehearsals, audio for video, and sound effects with your iPad. Mono and stereo mics were presented, along with the three common mic recording techniques: A-B, X-Y, and mid-side. A variety of microphones were presented at a variety of price points. The iPad can also help with audio analysis in concert venues and in home studios.

Chapter 6

AUDIO INTERFACES AND DOCKS

The equipment described in this chapter goes beyond the limitations of the hardware and apps described in chapter 5. This chapter focuses on reviewing the myriad of audio/MIDI interfaces for the iPad that support from 1 to 32 channels of audio input and can record in resolutions up to 96 kHz (kilohertz). The first questions to ask are how many inputs you need and what type of inputs. This chapter begins with single connector interfaces and progresses through devices with multiple inputs. After you choose the best audio interface for your needs, chapter 7 will address the apps you will need to make the iPad the center of your audio production studio, similar to Mac and PC computer applications.

Technical Terms

This section covers technical information and terms related to the cable connectors and sample rates mentioned in the descriptions to follow. If you are familiar with these terms, move ahead to the next section.

Cable Connectors

In chapter 5, the interfaces included one or more of the following connectors: 1/4-inch, 1/8-inch, and USB. The interfaces in this chapter have more connections and additional connector types. Below is a streamlined overview of the connectors mentioned. For more in-depth reading on the subject of wiring and connectors, pick up a copy of *Microphones and Mixers* (second edition) by Bill Gibson, published by Hal Leonard Books.

RCA connectors, also called *phono connectors*, were developed by the Radio Corporation of America and have been around since the early 1940s. They can carry both audio and video signals, and are most commonly found on the back panels of consumer audio and video equipment.

Figure 6.01. RCA connector.

TRS (or tip/ring/sleeve) connector is another name used to describe the 1/4-inch and 1/8-inch connectors mentioned throughout this book. Originally invented for telephone switchboards, these connectors carry both audio and video signals. There are variants of this connector. For example, the electric guitar or bass connector is a TS connector, with no ring. TRS connectors are used with stereo headphones. The tip carries the signal for mono connections, or just the left channel in stereo connections. The ring carries the right channel in stereo connections. The sleeve is the ground-absorbing, diffusing, and rejecting interference.

Figure 6.02. TRS connector.

XLR three-pin connectors are most commonly used with microphones. They are also used to connect pro audio equipment such as mixers and effects processors. XLR connectors are also used for AES/EBU digital audio connections (AES/EBU is a digital audio standard connection used to carry signal between digital audio devices. It was developed by the AES [Audio Engineering Society] and the EBU [European Broadcasting Union]).

Figure 6.03. XLR connector.

The combo connector allows you to connect either a 1/4-inch or XLR cable.

Figure 6.04. Combo connector.

TOSLINK (an acronym for Toshiba Link) is a fiber optical cable used in digital audio hardware such as DAT recorders, DVD and CD players, and video game consoles. The ports for TOSLINK connections are often labeled "Optical" on the back panels of equipment.

Figure 6.05. TOSLINK connector.

S/PDIF (Sony/Phillips Digital Interface Format) is the format of digital audio carried over optical TOSLINK cables or coaxial RCA cables. S/PDIF can carry two channels of digital audio.

ADAT, or ADAT Lightpipe, was developed by Alesis to carry eight tracks of digital audio at a resolution of 48 kHz/24-bit between ADAT digital tape recorders. The format was widely accepted and is still used by many third-party companies.

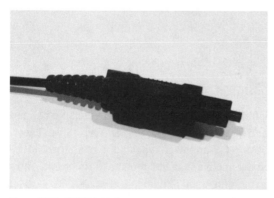

Figure 6.06. ADAT Lightpipe.

MIDI: In this chapter you will see both the original five-pin DIN MIDI connector and the USB MIDI connector. No audio information travels over MIDI cables—only note-on and note-off, velocity, duration, and controller data.

Figure 6.07. MIDI five-pin DIN connector.

D-sub 25-pin: The "D" in D-sub comes from the D shape of the metal shield around the connector's pins. Variants of this connector type include VGA and RGB. They are primarily used for multichannel analog and digital audio in professional recording studio gear.

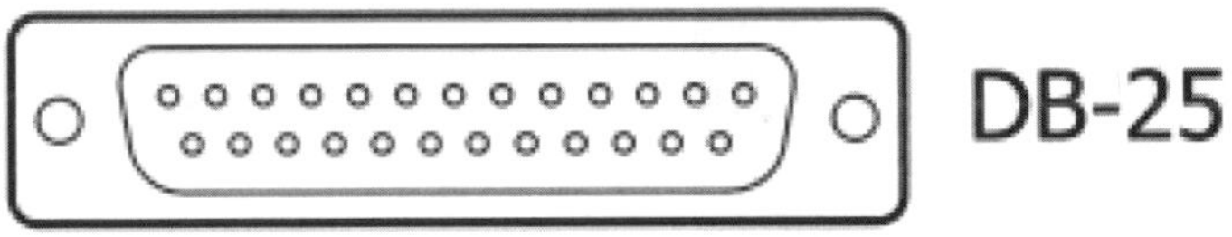

DB-25

Figure 6.08. D-sub 25-pin connector.

The BNC connector is a miniature quick connect/disconnect RF connector used for coaxial cable. BNC connectors are similar to the ones used to carry the signal to your cable TV box—just a little bulkier, and easier to quickly and securely connect. In the recording studio, they are used to transmit Word Clock to digital devices for precise synchronization.

Figure 6.09. BNC connector.

MADI (Multichannel Audio Digital Interface) is a format for carrying multiple channels of digital audio. MADI can be transmitted over coaxial cable or fiber optic cable. The number of tracks can be as many as 56 or 64 channels at resolutions of up to 96 kHz/24-bit. MADI is us j14126ed to link large studio mixers to digital multitrack recorders and converters, such as the Antelope Orion 32 mentioned later in this chapter.

Figure 6.10. MADI connector.

Recording Resolution Numbers

The most common recording resolutions used today are 48 kHz/24-bit and 96 kHz/24-bit. The first number is the *sampling rate*, which indicates the number of times per second that the source is sampled or recorded. CDs use a 44.1 kHz sample rate. For higher-quality recording, the sample rate is increased. Sample rates of 48 kHz, 96 kHz, and 192 kHz are used in audio production. Higher sample rate numbers also produce larger file sizes. As the price of file storage drops, higher sample rates have become popular and cost effective in desktop music production. Since iPad memory is fixed, you must be mindful of how much storage space is available before recording. Check the Usage tab in the Settings app to see how much empty space is available on your iPad (see chapter 1). If you are collaborating with someone, confirm before recording which resolutions he or she may be able to use.

The number after the sampling rate is the *bit depth*. The number of bits in each sample determine the audio dynamic range. Each bit adds 6 decibels to the dynamic range of the audio sample. The CD sampling rate of 44.1 kHz is done at a 16-bit depth. All digital recording hardware is capable of recording at this resolution and bit depth. For 48kHz and 96kHz sampling rates, the bit depth is increased to 24. As of this writing, the highest possible sample rate for the iPad is 96 kHz/24-bit. High-end computer-based recording systems such as Pro Tools HD are capable of recording using a 32-bit floating-point depth with a 192 kHz sampling rate (floating point = complex math!)

Types of Interfaces

Audio interfaces for the iPad currently on the market can be placed into one of the following four categories:

1. Interfaces built specifically for the iPad (made for iPad/iPhone/iPod or MFI, which stands for "made for iPad").
2. Interfaces that will work with the iPad and with a Mac or PC computer.
3. Interfaces that require the Apple Camera Connection Kit (abbreviated CCK).
4. Interfaces that require the Camera Connection Kit and a powered USB hub.

In order for hardware—such as interfaces, MIDI keyboards, and microphones—to work with the iPad, they must be either class compliant (see chapter 2) or MFI. The acronym MFI is starting to appear in product descriptions and reviews. MFI devices are those in categories 1 and 2 above, and they connect directly to either the iPad's 30-pin or Lightning connector, or the headphone jack. The majority of the interfaces described in this chapter are MFI devices; the few exceptions are indicated in the item description.

Some of these devices draw more power from USB than the iPad can provide. They can still be used but must be connected to a powered USB hub—and the hub connected to the Apple Camera Connector Kit.

> **Tip:** CCK devices do not charge the iPad while in use. You will need to figure recharging time into your workflow or use multiple iPads.

The first questions to ask are how many inputs you need and what types. This section begins with single connector interfaces and progresses through devices with multiple inputs.

Single Channel Audio Interfaces

With a single connector interface, you can connect one microphone or one electronic instrument such as a guitar or keyboard. In the mid-to-upper price range, these interfaces will support recording from both a mic and a 1/4-inch source to a single mono track at the same time. Most of these units also work with computers, so you can plug them into your iPad or computer and use them with appropriate software.

iRig Pre by IK Multimedia ($39.99)
www.ikmultimedia.com/products/irigpre/

iRig Pre is a single XLR input microphone preamp. A preamp increases the microphone's signal to line level. Plug in any dynamic, condenser, or ribbon mic (see chapter 5), and record to your iPad. The unit requires a 9-volt battery for power and has a switch for providing 48-volt power (phantom power) to condenser mics. There is a gain (volume) controller on the side and a 1/8-inch connector for headphones or connecting to an audio system for monitoring or playback. iRig Pre connects to the iPad though the headphone jack.

iRig Pre includes two free iPad apps from IK Multimedia to get started with your recording: iRig Recorder (see chapter 5) and VocaLive Free (mentioned in chapter 5 [page 111] of *Musical iPad*).

Figure 6.11. iRig Pre.

VIDEO 6.1. IRIG PRE DEMO.

Figure 6.12
http://youtu.be/V-_I5bJPEFg

iXZ by TASCAM ($69.99 list price)
http://tascam.com/product/ixz/overview/

iXZ is a light and portable interface that easily fits into a road case. It uses a single combo connector that accepts XLR and 1/4-inch inputs. A switch to the right of the connector configures the unit to accept the lower level signals from a guitar- or microphone-level input. A condenser mic requires 48-volt phantom power from the interface. The iXZ uses two AA batteries to supply phantom power to the mic. An indicator light on the top of the iXZ glows green when a mic is connected and dims when the batteries need to be changed. An input volume controller rounds out the unit's front panel. A 1/8-inch headphone jack is on the rear panel. The iXZ connects to the iPad's headphone jack.

Figure 0.13. iXZ.

VIDEO 6.2. IXZ DEMO.

Figure 6.14
http://youtu.be/D-YvHXCB9Po

iTrack Solo by Focusrite ($149.99 list price)
http://us.focusrite.com/ipad-audio-interfaces-usb-audio-interfaces/itrack-solo

iTrack Solo includes a preamplifier and has a microphone XLR connector and a 1/4-inch connector to record directly from electric and bass guitars. There are separate volume controls for each input. An LED light around the volume knob turns red when the input volume is too loud. The microphone input has a 48-volt power button for condenser mics. On the right side of the front panel are a large master volume control and a 1/4-inch connector for headphones. There is also a switch to turn on direct monitoring so you hear the signal directly from the iTrack's inputs—this means there is zero latency. There are two RCA jacks on the rear panel for connecting to a mixer or powered monitors.

Connection to the iPad requires a special cable, supplied with the unit. iTrack can be used with the app Tape by Focusrite (see chapter 5) for two-track recording, or with multitrack recording apps such as GarageBand or Auria (see chapter 7).

iTrack Solo is also fully compatible with a Mac or PC computer, and it comes with the computer software programs Abelton Live Lite and the Focusrite Scarlett Plug-in Suite. Focusrite also offers iTrack Studio for its $274.99 list price, which includes the iTrack Solo with a condenser microphone and headphones.

Figure 6.15. iTrack Solo.

VIDEO 6.3. ITRACK SOLO DEMO.

Figure 6.16
http://youtu.be/AEzqlx-37HE

Fast Track Solo by Avid ($179 list price)
www.avid.com/US/products/fasttrack-solo/features#overview

With the Fast Track Solo, you can connect a microphone and electronic instrument simultaneously and record in resolutions up to 48 kHz/24-bit. The front panel has inputs for a microphone XLR connector, a 1/4-inch connector for an electronic instrument, and a 1/4-inch connector for headphones.

Each input has a knob to control input volume and LEDs that change from green to red when the signal is too loud. Next to the headphone jack is a button to turn on direct monitoring so you can listen to the inputs of the Fast Track Solo with zero latency. There is a switch located on the rear panel of the unit to supply a condenser microphone with 48-volt phantom power, and there are two RCA connectors for sending the output to a mixer or powered speakers. The volume knob on the front panel controls both the level in the headphones and the level of the RCA outputs.

As of this writing, Avid does not have an iOS version of Pro Tools. However, the Fast Track Solo is a class compliant device that works with GarageBand, Auria, and other multitrack recording apps (see chapter 7). The Fast Track Solo can also function as a USB audio interface for Mac and PC computers. The added bonus is that the Mac and PC program Pro Tools Express is included, so you can edit and mix your tracks on your computer if you prefer.

Figure 6.17. Avid Fast Track Solo.

VIDEO 6.4. FAST TRACK SOLO DEMO.

Figure 6.18
http://youtu.be/3pZT34PC-y0

One by Apogee Digital ($349 list price)
www.apogeedigital.com/products/one.php

One by Apogee Digital combines an audio interface and microphone in one unit. Apogee Digital is known for the quality of its AD/DA converters, and One provides excellent audio quality in 44.1 kHz or 48 kHz resolution. There is a power cord provided for using it with the iPad. The power cord connects to the top of the interface and charges your iPad when connected. For portable use, there is a compartment on the back of the unit for two AA batteries.

One is also designed to be placed on a microphone stand. A special mic stand clip is included to position it appropriately for speaking or performing. The mic is located on the front of the unit in the center of the metal band, underneath the word *one*. Below the mic is a silver knob that controls input and output volume. LED meters are just above the knob. Press down on the knob to select the source for input, and the icons underneath the microphone will light up as each input is selected. An external mic or electronic instrument can be connected to One by using the provided breakout cable. The cable is attached to a connector on top of the unit and splits into connectors for one XLR and one 1/4-inch input. A 1/8-inch headphone connector is located on the bottom of the unit. One by Apogee can connect to a Mac using the USB cable. When connected to a MAC computer, it will draw power through USB and does not need a power cord.

Figure 6.19. One by Apogee Digital.

One by Apogee users can download the free app Apogee Maestro from the App Store. Maestro accesses One's internal settings and allows you operate the unit from your iPad. https://itunes.apple.com/us/app/apogee-maestro/id591261064?mt=8

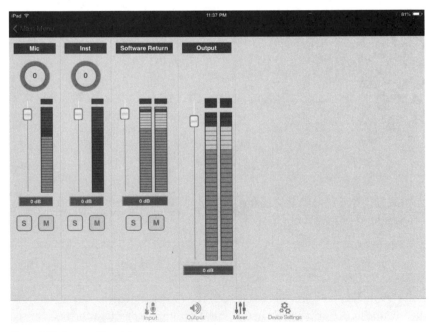

Figure 6.20. Apogee Maestro.

VIDEO 6.5. ONE BY APOGEE DIGITAL OVERVIEW.

Figure 6.21.
http://youtu.be/ArRhrl0UkKQ

Multichannel Interfaces

A multichannel interface can record on two or more separate tracks. The single input devices in the previous section can only record on one mono track. To record in stereo, you need a multichannel interface and two microphones (or one stereo microphone; see chapter 5), two preamps, and an app that allows for recording on two separate tracks (see chapter 7).

Multitrack Recording

In addition to recording on two tracks simultaneously, multichannel interfaces allow you to record at different times and layer two independent recordings. For example, you could record a duet by recording yourself singing the first part on track one and then going back and recording the second part on the second track. You would then mix the two tracks to create a stereo recording. This is called *multitrack recording*. Of course, more inputs mean more options and more equipment. At the very basic level, you'll need two microphones, as well as cables and mic stands).

> **Tip:** When purchasing two microphones for stereo recording, look for a matched set or "matched pair." A matched pair of mics will give you the best results. They can cost as little as $89.99 (list price) for a pair of Behringer C-2 small diaphragm condenser microphones, or thousands of dollars for a pair of AKG C414XL II/ST microphones ($3,299 list price).

Fast Track Duo by Avid ($299 list price)
www.avid.com/US/products/fasttrack-duo

The Fast Track Duo is a two-channel interface capable of recording up to 48 kHz/24-bit resolution. There are two combo connectors on the front panel, for XLR microphones or 1/4-inch cables from a guitar or bass. There are also two 1/4-inch input connectors on the rear panel of the unit for connecting electronic keyboards. There are two selector buttons on the front panel for selecting the front or rear inputs. Volume knobs on the front panel control the level for both sets of inputs. The Fast Track Duo has a Direct Monitor button so you can hear the signal from the unit's inputs with zero latency. Headphones connect to a 1/4-inch connector on the front panel and have a separate volume control knob. On the rear panel, there are two 1/4-inch outs for connecting to a mixer or powered speakers. The Fast Track Duo has a single switch to turn on 48-volt power, which activates phantom power for both combo jacks. There is a USB connector for use with Mac or PC computers, and a connector for a proprietary cable to connect to the iPad. Fast Track Duo comes with Pro Tools Express software for Mac or Windows. You will have to purchase an iPad DAW app in order to record on the iPad (see chapter 7).

Figure 6.22. Avid Fast Track Duo.

Duet by Apogee Digital ($595 list price)
www.apogeedigital.com/products/duet.php

Duet by Apogee is a two-channel interface that also includes a USB MIDI connector. Audio connections for Duet use a breakout cable, with two combo connectors for XLR or 1/4-inch inputs and two 1/4-inch outputs for connecting to powered monitors. A breakout cable connects to a single port on the interface and divides into multiple input and output connectors. MIDI devices must be Core MIDI-compatible to work with Duet (see chapter 2). When the Duet is used with the iPad, its power cord must be connected, as it powers the interface and charges the iPad at the same time. The Duet lies flat on the table when in use and has a rubberized bottom plate to keep it from sliding during operation. A breakout cable is used for connecting microphones and electronic instruments. If you prefer a hardware unit for connecting cables, a breakout box accessory is available as a $149 separate purchase. The Duet is capable of recording at resolutions of up to 192 kHz/24-bit.

Figure 6.23. Apogee Duo breakout box.

The top-panel interface consists of a color OLED (Organic Light Emitting Diode) display that shows metering, input grouping, phase, muting, phantom power, Soft Limit indication, and numeric value for input and output levels. Soft Limit is Apogee's technology for preventing peaks in the volume level from distorting when they reach the A/D converter in the signal chain. A silver multifunction knob on the top cycles though the input options when pressed and sets volume levels by turning right or left.

The two white circles above the knob are configurable touch pads that can be assigned to tasks such as "mute outputs" or "toggle headphone source." Apogee's free Maestro app for the iPad can also be used to control all of Duet's settings.

There is a 1/4-inch headphone jack on the bottom of the unit. You can create two separate mixes with the Duet and send one to the I/O output and another to the headphone outputs. In live performance, a band can use prerecorded tracks, sending a click track to the monitors and the other track to a house sound system. Or a DJ can monitor a separate mix in the headphones while sending a house mix to the club (see chapter 4).

Duet is compatible only with Mac computers. An OSX computer version of Maestro is available to access the interface's controls.

Figure 6.24. Apogee Digital Duet.

VIDEO 6.6. DUET BY APOGEE DIGITAL OVERVIEW.

Figure 6.25
http://youtu.be/HJtigSQS-Z8

iConnectAUDIO4+ by iConnectivity
www.iconnectivity.com/iConnectAudio4plus

iConnectAudio4+ is a four-input audio interface capable of recording up to 96 kHz/24-bit. It is USB and MIDI class compliant and will charge the iPad while connected. The front panel has four combo jacks for XLR or 1/4-inch inputs. Next to the inputs is a captive touch display; touch the parameter you wish to control, and the knob to the right of the display adjusts the values. The rear panel has 1/4-inch connectors for headphones and four individual outputs. If you want to use powered monitors (see chapter 7), you must use two outputs or a Y-split cable from the headphone connector.

There are two five-pin DIN MIDI connectors for MIDI IN and MIDI OUT to connect a powered MIDI device. A USB connector labeled "Host" enables the connection of a USB hub where you can connect multiple USB MIDI devices. There are two USB connectors on the rear panel. You can connect two computing devices—for example, an iPad and a computer. There is a switch to select the connections you wish to use on the rear panel. iConnectivity's Audio passThru™ technology allows you to route audio digitally between two computing devices. iConnectAUDIO4+ also works with Mac and PC computers. The iConfig app and software will handle device setup and routing on the iPad, and on Mac and PC computers.

Figure 6.26. iConnectAUDIO4+.

VIDEO 6.7. ICONNECTAUDIO4+ DEMO.

Figure 6.27
http://youtu.be/dbb0EYZH3zg

Quartet by Apogee Digital ($1,395)
www.apogeedigital.com/products/quartet.php

The Quartet builds on the technology of Apogee's Duet interface (mentioned previously in this chapter), increasing the connectivity and versatility in recording and audio production. The Quartet's back panel has four combo connectors for microphones or electronic instruments. There are six 1/4-inch output connectors that can be used as individual outputs, paired as three stereo outputs to feed to different monitors, or used to provide 5.1 output for surround sound playback. Two ADAT optical inputs allow connection of other A/D converters, such as Apogee's Ensemble, which adds eight additional input channels. A WC Out port for a BNC connector allows additional digital devices (such as A/D converters) to be synced using Quartet's internal clock. A USB class compliant MIDI keyboard or DJ controller can be connected. The power cable connector must be used when connected to the iPad. A 1/4-inch headphone jack is located on the right side of the unit.

The Quartet has an OLED panel that displays mctcr levels and numeric values for input levels. A multifunction control knob cycles through the settings options when pressed and can change volume levels for input and output. Quick Touch pads, including three that are user-assignable, are used to access recording and monitoring functions. Apogee's free Maestro app can be used to control all of the Quartet's settings. Quartet is compatible with Mac computers, and there is a software version of Maestro to access Quartet's settings from a Mac.

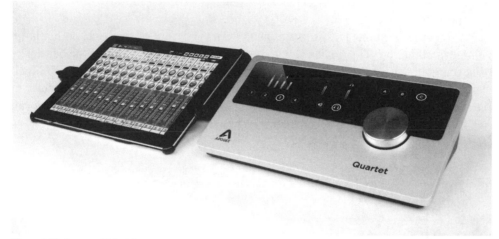

Figure 6.28. Apogee Digital Quartet.

VIDEO 6.8. QUARTET BY APOGEE DIGITAL DEMO.

Figure 6.29
http://youtu.be/RbXerwAeCIQ

iPad Docks

A dock is a hardware device that connects both your iPad and other gear in your music studio, such as an electric guitar, MIDI gear, and speakers/headphones. Docks provide more connection options than most stand-alone interfaces mentioned previously in this chapter. Connect the iPad to the dock, launch your favorite recording app (see chapter 7), and you are ready to go. When you are finished, there is no need to disconnect anything, other than removing the iPad from the dock. Your studio gear remains connected for the next session.

Docks are well worth considering as the hub of an iPad studio. Since there are different shapes and sizes of iPads (see chapter 1), check the dock's compatibility with the specific model you own before purchasing. And be sure that it is secure while you tap and swipe on the iPad screen. If you're considering purchasing a new iPad, make sure the model is compatible with the dock.

Studio Connect by Griffin Technology ($99.99 list price)
http://store.griffintechnology.com/studioconnect-na17132

Studio Connect is a lightweight, cradle-style dock that comes in two models: the original, for 30-pin iPads, and a Lightning connector model. The dock connects to the iPad using a supplied cable that will also charge the iPad when connected. Studio Connect can record up to two tracks simultaneously. This can be a single stereo recording or multiple mono tracks. MIDI can be recorded along with audio on a separate MIDI track.

A 1/8-inch headphone jack is positioned at the very front of the base, with a large volume knob on top. The input volume controller is on the right side of the base. The back panel has a 1/4-inch mono connector for electric guitar or bass and a 1/8-inch stereo input for electronic keyboard. There are two five-pin DIN MIDI connectors in the middle of the back panel, but no USB MIDI connectors. Two RCA connectors can link the Studio Connect to powered monitors or a mixer.

Figure 6.30. Studio Connect.

Studio Connect HD by Griffin Technology ($199.99)
http://store.griffintechnology.com/studioconnect-hd

Studio Connect's new big brother is the Studio Connect HD. HD refers to the recording resolution of 96 kHz/24-bit. The Studio Connect can record two tracks simultaneously, but the resolution is set in the app and may be limited to what resolutions the app supports (see chapter 7). MIDI can be recorded along with audio to a separate MIDI track.

The Studio Connect HD uses a cradle dock designed to hold the iPad at a higher angle than either the Alesis or Focusrite docks mentioned later in this chapter. The base has two combo connectors on the front for microphones or electronic instrument cables. The input volume controls are on the top panels, over the input connectors. Two switches for 48-volt phantom power are also on top. A 1/4-inch headphone connector is conveniently placed on the front panel. The back panel has connectors for both five-pin DIN MIDI connectors and USB MIDI connectors, with in and out connections for each type. Two 1/4-inch outputs route Studio Connect's audio to powered speakers or a mixer. Cables are included for 30-pin and Lightning iPads. The Studio Connect HD can also be used as a USB interface with Mac computers via the supplied cable; it is not compatible with PC computers.

Figure 6.31. Studio Connect HD.

iO Dock II by Alesis ($299)
www.alesis.com/io-dock-ii

Alesis was the first company to bring an iPad dock to the market and then feel the effects of the change from 30-pin to Lightning connectors. To address iPads with 30-pin or Lightning connectors, the redesigned iO Dock II uses a cable with a switchable adapter. A height adjustment sled is also included for the thinner iPad Air so that it fits snugly in the dock.

The inputs are located on the back panel. They include two combo connectors to handle mic and line level audio signals, each with its own volume control knobs. Input 1 has a switch for selecting guitar or line level for the signal. A single switch sends phantom power to both combo inputs. There are two 1/4-inch outputs for connecting to monitors or a mixer, and a switch to enable direct monitoring of the recording source with zero latency. Two tracks can be recorded simultaneously to any audio recording app. The iO Dock II has 24-bit converters, but the maximum resolution possible depends on the recording app.

Guitarists will find the footswitch input a bonus. It can be used to connect a pedal to control a guitar effects app on the iPad (see chapter 3), or a footswitch that sends MIDI messages to an app so that the transport and recording controls can be accessed without touching the iPad.

On the left side of the unit, you can connect MIDI devices by using the two five-pin DIN MIDI connectors: MIDI in and MIDI out. There is a USB MIDI connector for sending MIDI data to and from a computer. Volume control for the main outputs is located on the right side of the unit, along with the headphone connector. There is a separate control knob for headphone volume level. The iO Dock II places the iPad at a low angle and holds it firmly enough that energetic tapping on the screen, such as when playing percussion parts, will not cause a problem.

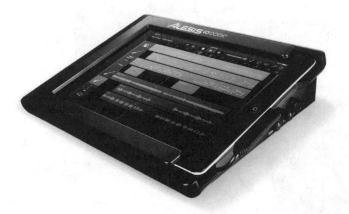

Figure 6.32. iO Dock II.

VIDEO 6.9. IO DOCK II OVERVIEW.

Figure 6.33
http://youtu.be/yG3vECq1-BE

iTrack Dock by Focusrite ($ 249.99 list price)
http://us.focusrite.com/ipad-audio-interfaces/itrack-dock#overview

The iTrack Dock was the first dock both to feature the Lightning connector and designed to accommodate the iPad Mini as well as the full sized iPad. This dock is not compatible with the 30-pin iPad models—only fourth-generation iPads (or newer) and the iPad Mini. The iTrack can record at resolutions up to 96 kHz/24-bit, but check the settings of your audio recording app to see what resolutions it supports.

The dock's Lightning connector is located on the left side of the tray, and it slides to accommodate the full-size iPad or the iPad Mini. The top panel has separate volume controllers for each of the two inputs. The base of each knob is surrounded by Focusrite's halo LEDs, which turn red when the volume is too loud. There is a direct monitoring button for no-latency monitoring of the input signal. A small silver knob controls the headphone volume; a large knob controls the main output volume. The back panel has two XLR connectors for mic inputs. A single switch turns on 48-volt phantom power for both XLR inputs. There are three 1/4-inch connectors, one instrument input for electric guitar or bass, and two line level inputs for electronic keyboards. A single USB MIDI connector handles a keyboard or another MIDI controller device, such as percussion pads.

You can record using Tape by Focusrite (see chapter 5), a free two-track recording app available in the App Store, or multitrack DAW apps such as GarageBand, Cubasis, or Auria (see chapter 7).

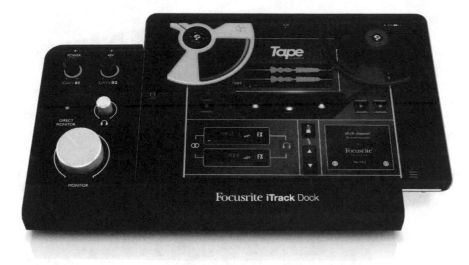

Figure 6.34. iTrack Dock Top.

iO Mix by Alesis ($399 list price)
www.alesis.com/io-mix

iO Mix dock can record four simultaneous tracks. It has a mixer as part of the hardware dock and a video out. The unit includes connectors for 30-pin and Lightning iPads and locks the iPad securely in place with a hinged door. It has four combo input connectors on the rear panel. Channel 1 can switch between instrument and line level for guitars or keyboards respectively. When using condenser mics, 48-volt phantom power can be applied to the inputs in pairs. The power switch is located between the pair of inputs it controls. Each channel has a high-pass filter switch that, when activated, reduces the amount of low frequencies recorded for eliminating unwanted noise. A pair of 1/4-inch outputs connects the iO Mix to an audio system or powered monitors.

On the top panel, there are four mixer channels, each with its own volume slider, panning controller, and Hi and Low EQ controller. There are LEDs on each channel to indicate volume peaks. The mixer is capable of routing audio from each of the four inputs to four separate tracks in a DAW app (see chapter 7). With the press of a button, you can convert the inputs to a stereo pair of tracks. There is a volume fader for the main outputs and a knob to control the headphone level. The headphone connector is on the front of the device, on the right side. There is a Direct button to monitor the inputs of the iO Mix mix directly, with zero latency. A component video and an S-VHS jack are located on the rear panel to connect to a projector, monitor, or TV. This enables the iPad's screen to be displayed on a larger screen for video presentations, entertainment, or educational applications.

Figure 6.35. iO Mix.

Apple Camera Connection Kit Interfaces

Multichannel interfaces that require the Apple Camera Connection Kit are typically made for use with desktop and laptop computers. With Core Audio being used in both the Mac OSX and iOS operating systems, these USB class compliant devices can be recognized by the iPad as long as you have the Apple Camera Connection Kit (see chapter 2).

Some interfaces work using only the Camera Connection Kit; others must be linked to the camera connector through a powered USB hub. This technique allows many interfaces to connect with the iPad; however, not all apps work with interfaces connected in this manner, so be sure to test them before purchasing. Also, none of the current CCK interfaces charge the iPad while connected. WaveMachine Labs maintains a list of audio interfaces that are known to work with Auria on their website: http://auriaapp.com/Support/auria-audio-interfaces.

Four is the maximum number of inputs currently available for recording to an iPad with a MFI interface. If you require more inputs, a CCK device is the only solution.

AudioBox 1818VSL by PreSonus ($629 list price)
www.presonus.com/products/AudioBox-1818VSL

The AudioBox 1818VSL is an eight-channel USB interface that connects to the iPad by routing the unit's USB cable to a powered USB hub and then plugging the USB hub to the iPad (see Video 6.10). The 1818VSL has eight combo jacks on the front panel. Input volume controls are stacked in two rows to the right of the inputs; the main and headphone output volume are on the far right. There are two buttons to the left of the combo connectors that enable 48-volt phantom power in groups of four.

The back panel has individual 1/4-inch outputs for all eight channels for routing to a mixer, and a pair of main 1/4-inch outs for sending to a mixer or powered monitors. The 181VSL also has five-pin DIN MIDI IN and OUT connectors. There are S/PDIF and ADAT audio connectors and a BNC connector for Word Clock syncing.

Figure 6.36. Auria Input Matrix.

Tip: The AudioBox 1818VSL is also a USB interface for Mac and PC computers, and it comes with PreSonus Studio One computer DAW software. The iPad can be used to control the unit's internal mixer remotely (see chapter 8).

Connecting an MFI and CCK Interface

The differences between connecting an MFI interface and a CCK interface were mentioned earlier in the chapter. In this video, the Apogee Duet, an MFI interface, and the PreSonus AudioBox 1818VSL (a CCK interface) are connected to the iPad. Connecting to GarageBand, Cubasis, and Auria are demonstrated.

Figure 6.37. PreSonus 1818VSL.

VIDEO 6.10. CONNECTING AN MFI AND CCK INTERFACE.

Figure 6.38
https://vimeo.com/87882920

Specialized Devices

Not all iPad-related devices fit neatly into categories. The devices in this section perform a specific role handling audio for the iPad. Both bypass the internal A/D converters of the iPad, substituting their own for higher-quality audio reproduction.

iD100 Digital Dock for iPad & iPhone by Cambridge Audio ($329 list price)
www.cambridgeaudio.com/products/id100-digital-dock-for-ipad-iphone

The iD100 is designed to connect the iPad to a high-quality home entertainment system via a digital connection. It has a single XLR output for an AES/EBU connection, a TOSLINK optical output, a S/PDIF coaxial output, and a video out. This is not an interface that can be used for recording, only playback. The iD100 takes a digital signal out of the iPad, bypassing its internal converter and using the iD100's higher-quality converter.

This device is designed for listening to your tracks and mixes on a high-quality stereo or AV system for testing or entertainment. If a stereo receiver or amplifier is not available, or does not have a digital input connector, Cambridge offers the DacMagic 100 D/A Converter ($399 list price) that connects to the dock and provides two RAC outputs to connect to an audio system or powered monitors.

Figure 6.39. iD100.

VIDEO 6.11. ID100 DIGITAL DOCK OVERVIEW.

Figure 6.40
http://youtu.be/DFhwn2VyEWo

Orion 32 by Antelope Audio ($2,995)

http://antelopeaudio.com/en/products/Orion32-Multi-Channel-AD-DA-converter

The Orion 32 is a 32-channel A/D converter designed for the professional recording studio. It is not an interface with 1/4-inch and XLR inputs; rather, it connects to large mixers, multichannel preamps, or digital interfaces using D-sub 25-pin, ADAT Lightpipe, or MADI connectors. For example, it is possible to bypass the A/D converters in an Avid Pro Tools interface. Then, you can route the audio from the Avid interface's inputs to the Orion 32's inputs, using the Orion's circuitry to convert the audio to digital for recording.

The Orion 32 connects to the iPad through the Apple Camera Connection Kit. As the name implies, the unit can input and output 32 tracks of audio when connected to a computer. Currently the maximum track count available when recording on the iPad, using the Auria app (see chapter 7), is 24 tracks. Once the iPad is connected to the Orion 32, the Orion's inputs and outputs will be available for assignment in Auria.

As of this writing, this is the top of the line for recording audio on the iPad and an option for large studios and multichannel DAW owners who want to use the iPad as the center of a professional recording studio. Mobile rigs will benefit the most from the addition of an iPad, as it is lighter than computer desktops or laptops and has no fan noise. On the down side, the Orion 32 does not charge the iPad while in use, so charging may be required during long sessions unless multiple iPads are used.

Figure 6.41. Orion 32.

VIDEO 6.12. ORION 32.

Figure 6.42
http://youtu.be/p0G7AB40GpE

Studios

Deciding which interface best suits your needs today is fairly simple. However, consider where you'd like to be in the next three to five years. If you want something just to record song demos, a single input interface may be all you need. These studios are broken down by hardware type and number of inputs.

Single Channel Audio Recording (Option 1)

This includes all devices in the single input category.

- iPad 2 or later: starting at $499.00
- Interface: $39.99–$349.00

Total cost including iPad: $538.99–$848.00

Two Channel Audio Recording (Option 2)

This includes all interfaces with two inputs, excluding docks.

- iPad 2 or later: starting at $499.00
- Interface: $299.00–$595.00

Total cost including iPad: $798.00–$1,094.00

Four Channel Audio Recording (Option 3)

This includes both four input interfaces and the iO mix.

- iPad 2 or later: starting at $499.00
- Interface: $399.00–$1,395.00

Total cost including iPad: $898.00–$1,894.00

8 to 24 Channel Audio Recording (Option 4)

The prices only include the interfaces. For the PreSonus, you will need to purchase a powered MIDI hub. For the Orion 32, you will need the Apple Camera Connection Kit as well as a mixer, preamp bank, or audio interface to route audio into Orion's converters and the iPad.

- iPad 2 or later: starting at $499.00
- Interface: $629.00–$2995.00

Total cost including iPad: $1,128.00–$3,494.00

Dock Studio (Option 5)

This includes only Dock devices.

- iPad 2 or later: starting at $499.00
- Interface: $149.99–$399.00

Total cost including iPad: $648.99–$898.00

Chapter 6 Activities

1. Create a plan for developing your studio recording needs by answering the following questions:
   a. What recording and computer equipment do you already own?
   b. Do you already own an iPad? If yes, what generation and how much RAM?
   c. Would you like to record your rehearsals and concerts?
   d. Do you want the ability to record tracks in your home or road studio that can be used in the final mix of a song?
   e. Are you interested in learning more about microphone techniques and editing and mixing audio?
2. List the equipment you own, and look for new gear that is compatible with your existing gear.
3. Create a budget for purchasing the necessary equipment. Be honest about what your needs are, but do think about the kind of recording work you hope to be doing in the next few years. Then revisit the budget. Plan your acquisitions in stages if possible. If you own an older iPad, think about upgrading in three- to five-year intervals. You can sell your old iPad and use that cash toward an upgrade or keep it as a backup.
4. Choose the best interface for your studio. In the next chapter, you will look at apps for multitrack recording, so take the studio ideas from this chapter and add another line to the budget; then revisit the budget.

Summary

In this chapter, we began by examining the options for connecting digital audio equipment. We reviewed interface options for digital recording, beginning with single channel and including interfaces that record a single channel from two inputs, then moving on to multichannel interfaces with two, four and eight inputs. These interfaces record high-definition audio and accept MIDI input to control synth and percussion apps. On the high end, there are interfaces that can route up to 24 tracks of high-definition audio to the iPad for the ultimate in iOS recording.

With all of the options available, it takes careful analysis of current and near-term projection needs to choose the right interface. With the hardware in place, you can move on to chapter 8 and choose your software.

Chapter **7**
MULTITRACK
RECORDING

This chapter focuses on using the iPad with multitrack software for recording, editing, and mastering your music, and making the iPad the center of your music studio for creating and editing tracks. The apps listed can do much of what computer-based software can do, and they are designed specifically for the iPad. This chapter will also address options for integrating apps using Audiobus and Inter-App technology. Studio monitors for playback will be covered, along with file storage options. Using the iPad as an extension of a computer-based multitrack recording program is addressed in chapter 8.

Figure 7.1 Sample iPad-Based Studio.

DAW Defined

The apps mentioned in this chapter are referred to as a DAW (rhymes with "paw") or *digital audio workstation*. Another common term in the industry is *music production software*. Essentially, the focus is on sound and the final product being a mixed and mastered audio track. The two terms, DAW and music production software, are interchangeable. DAWs come in several different types, some specializing in synthesizer and sampling, while others focus just on recording live audio. And a third category tries to include all of the options—synth, sampler, and audio recording—in one app.

iPad DAW Apps

iPad DAW apps are similar to those in the Mac and Windows computer world: some are designed for novice musicians, while others are intended to be used by recording professionals. However, unlike computer software, iPad DAW apps are more specialized and much less expensive than their computer counterparts. If you are planning to make the iPad the center of your music studio, then you might consider purchasing two or more apps mentioned in this chapter, so you will have all of the features that you need and the ability to use the app that best suits a particular project.

What Do iPad DAW Apps Have in Common?

Before we explore the various options for DAW iPad apps, there are some things that they all have in common. Specifically, you can:

1. Connect a MIDI keyboard for note entry (see chapter 2).
2. Use Audiobus or Inter-App Audio with compatible apps to take advantage of one app's features, such as sound output or effects (covered later in this chapter).

Figure 7.2. iPad, mic, guitar and pedalboard.

What Don't iPad DAW Apps Have in Common?

Unlike computer software DAWS, iPad apps run the gamut and are not all the same. Review the following lists for an overview.

1. Some apps allow for the recording of audio, so you can use single input and multiple input devices to connect microphones for recording (see chapters 5 and 6).

2. Some apps allow for connecting an electric guitar, bass, or other electronic instrument (see chapter 3).

3. Some apps include just software instruments and loops, while others specialize in audio recording.

Fortunately, iPad apps are relatively inexpensive, so you can conceivably purchase several DAW apps for specific applications and use the one that best fits the project.

Audio and MIDI Utilities

The next few apps are for the higher-end users who want to combine multiple apps to incorporate audio and MIDI. The terms are placed here so that they are familiar to you when you read them in the app descriptions that follow.

Live Audio Streaming between Apps via Inter-App Audio and Audiobus

Audiobus was mentioned in chapter 3 of this book, as well as in chapter 3 of the *Musical iPad* (pages 69 and 70). Since that was written, Apple has come out with its own version of recording audio from one app to another: Inter-App Audio, which is built into iOS7 and later. Both Audiobus and Inter-App Audio serve as a connector between the output of one app and the input of another. They allow for live audio streaming between apps, making it possible to use apps together like modules in a recording studio. And with both options, you can route audio through a third (effects) app for sound processing.

Audiobus and Inter-App Audio are both APIs, or *application programming interfaces*, for iPad app developers to include in their own apps. Not all apps support Audiobus and Inter-App Audio, so check the app's specs before you purchase. A list of supported Audiobus apps is available at http://audiob.us/apps, and Inter-App Audio at http://www.ipadmusic.com/blog/2013/09/20/inter-app-audio/.

Inter-App Audio by Apple (built-in feature in iOS7 and later)

Inter-App Audio makes it possible to stream music between apps, but it is not an app itself. It is part of iOS7, so nothing needs to be installed or downloaded. You must be running iOS7 or later in order to use Inter-App Audio.

Inter-App Audio is making it possible to stream audio between apps. It is designed to work with a multitrack recording app, such as GarageBand or Cubasis and the other apps reviewed in this chapter. That app serves as the host. Then you can connect other apps—for example, to use a synth app such as Amplitude for additional sounds.

The option to use Inter-App Audio is available only when at least one other app that is compatible with Inter-App Audio is installed on your device. For example, with the multitrack app GarageBand, when you choose an instrument, one of the options is Inter-App Audio. When you tap on Inter-App Audio, a list of installed and compatible inter-app apps on your iPad will be displayed. Not every app supports Inter-App Audio. However, the number of compatible apps is growing all the time.

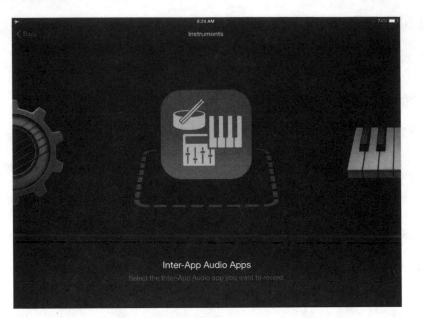

Figure 7.3 Inter-App Audio in GarageBand.

VIDEO 7.1 INTER-APP AUDIO DEMO.

Figure 7.4
http://youtu.be/4T5D1cD3RyQ

Audiobus by A Tasty Pixel ($4.99/in-app purchase available)

https://itunes.apple.com/us/app/audiobus/id558513570?mt=8

Audiobus is a third-party app that does the same job as Inter-App Audio, reviewed above. Namely, it allows audio to stream between apps. The advantage of using Audiobus is it will run with iOS5 or later, so you can use it on older iPads. Audiobus has three boxes: Input, Effects, and Output. Tap on any box, and a list of supporting apps pops up; select the desired app; then tap again to launch the app and be transferred to it for further setup. Load one app, and a plus sign is added above the Input box, indicating that you can layer input sounds, either with two apps or with a vocal input.

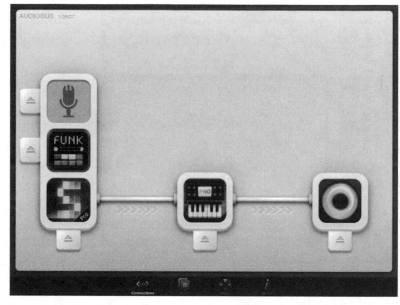

Figure 7.5. Audiobus sample screen.

VIDEO 7.2 AUDIOBUS DEMO.

Figure 7.6
http://youtu.be/map8L38ErPI

MIDI Utility: MidiBridge

MidiBridge by Audeonic Apps ($8.99)

https://itunes.apple.com/us/app/midibridgo/id440160850?mt=8

MidiBridge is the comprehensive MIDI tool that iOS is missing, and it is essential for anyone using MIDI devices with an iPad. It's a virtual MIDI patchbay and router that interconnects all MIDI interfaces (external, virtual, and network) on an iOS device. Whether from other apps where the developers have made their MIDI in/out visible, MIDI hardware connected to your device, or MIDI ins/outs available over a network, it provides a visual representation of all available MIDI inputs (sources) and outputs (destinations). In principle, this is all very straightforward, although there may also be a MIDI setting or two that needs configuring in the source/destination app itself to actually get the data flowing as required. For a complete review of this app, consult www.musicappblog.com/midi-bridge-app-review/.

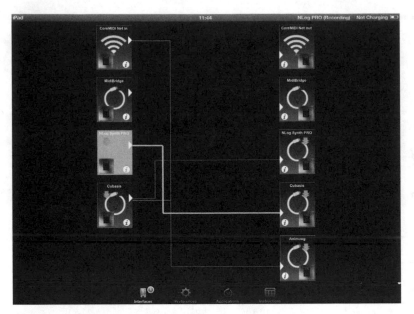

Figure 7.7. MidiBridge.

VIDEO 7.3 MIDIBRIDGE DEMO.

Figure 7.8
http://youtu.be/IV5hxGRTtmc

Multitrack Recording Apps

In this section, some of the popular iPad DAW apps are included. The cost of iPad apps is significantly less than that of computer DAW software, making it feasible to purchase multiple apps for your iPad-based studio. And with Inter-App Audio or Audiobus, multiple apps can be used together, expanding the options. The DAW apps are divided into three categories:

1. Synth (MIDI), drum, and sampler tracks
2. Audio tracks
3. Audio, synth (MIDI), and sampler tracks

Synth (MIDI), Drum, and Sampler Tracks

If your primary goal is to create tracks using synths and samplers, then consider one of the two apps included in this section: NanoStudio and Beatmaker 2. With NanoStudio, you can't record separate tracks of audio, but you can sample audio of various lengths. Beatmaker 2 includes an excellent drumbeat creator, synths, and sampler, as well as the capacity to record audio tracks. Both apps are geared toward electronic music, synthesis, and beat making.

NanoStudio by Blip Interactive Ltd. ($13.99 for 6 tracks/in-app purchase of $4.99 for an additional 10 tracks)
https://itunes.apple.com/us/app/nanostudio/id382263651?mt=8

NanoStudio reminds me of the program Reason by Propellerheads for Mac and PC computers, insofar as it has virtual analog synths, sample trigger pads, a comprehensive sequencer, and a sample editor. In addition, a mixer and multiple effects are integrated into the app, so you can complete your project from start to finish. You can record your ideas in real time, mix synth layers with samples, and add effects such as reverb, compression, and EQ. Share your finished project on SoundCloud from wherever you are, or use the audio mixdown options and MIDI export feature to export to other iPad apps or your Mac or PC computer.

Figure 7.9 NanoStudio SoundCloud posts
https://soundcloud.com/groups/nanostudio-official

NanoStudio is Audiobus compliant, so you can use other apps to record and add effects to your projects. You can't record vocals as full audio tracks, but you can sample short vocal parts (up to about 20 seconds) using the sample editor. You can check out some tracks developed using NanoStudio on the NanoStudio SoundCloud group:

If you want to add vocals beyond a 20-second sample to your NanoStudio composition, you could export the final mix of your project from NanoStudio to one of the iPad DAW apps that do record audio, such as GarageBand, Multitrack DAW, Cubasis, Auria and others mentioned later in this chapter; or export the file to one of your Mac- or PC-based DAW programs.

Figure 7.10. NanoStudio.

VIDEO 7.4 NANOSTUDIO DEMO.

Figure 7.11
http://youtu.be/KCXqC_mEdd0

Beatmaker 2 ($19.99/in-app purchases to add additional sounds and loops)
https://itunes.apple.com/us/app/beatmaker-2/id417020234?mt=8

Beatmaker has been around for a while on the iPad and iPhone. The Beatmaker 2 version added a lot of new features. It is Audiobus compliant and includes a host of music-making tools, and it could easily function as your main iPad DAW.

The built-in drum machine is an Akai MPC clone with 16 pads and a host of tweakable parameters for each pad. The drum machine portion of the app includes many sample drum kits for you to use as-is, or you can mix and match between individual samples from each kit.

Figure 7.12. Beatmaker 2 drum machine.

There is also support for a sampling keyboard instrument, so you can play along to your recorded beats. With the sampling recorder and editor, you can record samples via the iPad's built-in microphone or the headphone jack. The sequencer section adds a classic MIDI sequencer. Effects are available on both individual channels and the master output.

And in addition to drum machine, sampler, and sequencer, you can also record audio tracks. You can record multiple tracks simultaneously and use audio interfaces as described in chapters 5 and 6. For a complete list of specifications go to http://intua. net/products/beatmaker2/#specifications.

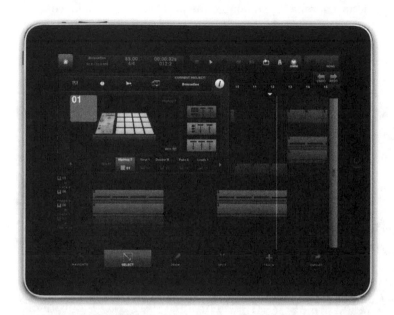

Figure 7.13. Beatmaker 2.

VIDEO 7.5 BEATMAKER 2 DEMO.

Figure 7.14
http://youtu.be/gBeSjsbVW18

Audio Tracks

If you are looking for a solution on the iPad to just record audio, there are several options. You can use the built-in iPad microphone or connect external mics to the iPad as described in chapters 5 and 6. There are two apps featured in this section: Multitrack DAW and Auria.

MultiTrack DAW by Harmonicdog
($9.99 for 8 tracks/in-app purchase to add an additional 8 tracks [$5.99] or 16 tracks [$7.99] for a total of 16 or 24 tracks respectively)
https://itunes.apple.com/US/app/id329322101?mt=8

MultiTrack DAW is a powerful audio recorder and editor. It does not include software instrument support or MIDI, but if audio recording and looping is your main objective, this is a powerful app. It is compatible with Audiobus, and you can use USB audio interfaces to facilitate connecting external microphones (see chapter 5) and other music gear, so it could be one of the main apps in your iPad-based studio. The initial app purchase of $9.99 will give you a maximum of 8 tracks. You can increase the total number of tracks via in-app purchase. To double the number to 16 tracks costs an additional $5.99, and to add 16 tracks for a total of 24 costs an additional $7.99. The app comes with some excellent mixing options, which include individual track and mastering EQ, compressor, reverb, and a flexible delay.

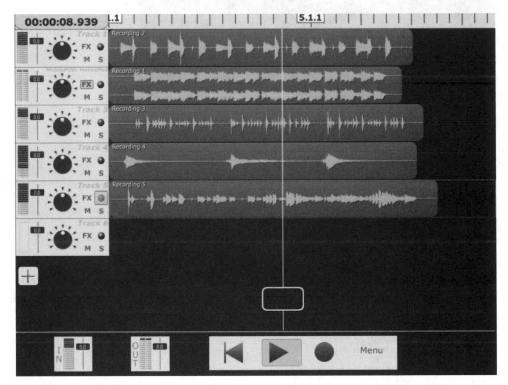

Figure 7.15 MultiTrack DAW.

VIDEO 7.6. MULTITRACK DAW DEMO.

Figure 7.16
http://youtu.be/fNN-y9ew_7A

Auria LE by WaveMachine Labs Inc. ($24.99/in-app purchases available)

https://itunes.apple.com/us/app/auria-le/id585683569?mt=8

Auria by WaveMachine Labs Inc. ($49.99/in-app purchases available)

http://auriaapp.com/

Auria has made a big splash as the "Pro Tools of the iPad." If you are unfamiliar with the term *Pro Tools*, check out http://en.wikipedia.org/wiki/Pro_Tools.

Auria LE has 8 tracks of simultaneous recording and 24 tracks of playback. The full version has 24 tracks of simultaneous recording and 48 tracks of playback. You could start with the LE version, as there is an in-app purchase to upgrade to the full version. The feature list of this app is impressive. Auria's architecture ensures ample headroom for plug-in processing and mixing/mastering, transforming your iPad into a recording and mixing studio with sound quality that rivals most computer-based DAWs. There are built-in effects and many optional add-on effects via in-app purchases engineered by PSPaudioware, Overloud, FabFilter, and Drumagog, and there is support for Dropbox, Soundcloud, AAF, and MP3. Auria raises the bar for recording and mixing on the iPad.

Auria provides the option of adding a video import feature via an in-app purchase of $4.99. It can also sync video to an Auria project. Adjustable offset times and video export capability is included, so you can use Auria to score to video. For a complete Auria feature list, check out http://auriaapp.com/Products/auria#AuriaFeatureList.

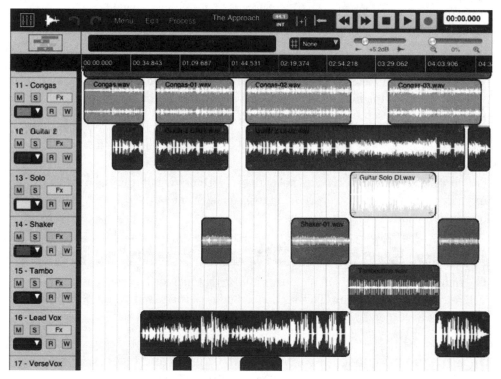

Figure 7.17 Auria Editor window.

VIDEO 7.7 DAVID KAHNE TALKS ABOUT AURIA.

Figure 7.18
http://youtu.be/D-83l1z96hl

For additional Auria demo videos, consult http://auriaapp.com/Products/auria-videos.

Inter-App Audio and Auria

What you won't find in Auria are synth tracks, virtual instruments, or a sampler. However, since it supports Inter-App Audio and Audiobus, you can record from one app into an Auria track. This will give you access to your synth apps and other sounds you may want to add to a project.

AuriaLink

WaveMachine Labs, the developers of Auria, have also implemented their own version of Bluetooth-based synchronization called AuriaLink. This allows you to sync two iPads that are both running Auria, providing a total of 96 tracks and intelligent linking of transport, scrolling, zooming, and resizing tracks. Start and stop messages will be automatically sent so that the slave device automatically follows the master; therefore, the transport is unavailable on the slave. Fast-forwarding and rewinding are synced as well, and because the Edit windows are linked, scrubbing the Timeline cursor on the master device will scrub the cursor on the slave too. AuriaLink is only available on the full version of Auria, not the LE version.

Auria and MIDI

The current version of Auria does not support MIDI or virtual tracks. So if MIDI input and editing are things you are looking for, consider one of the other apps mentioned later in this chapter, such as Cubasis.

Audio, Synth (MIDI), and Sampler Tracks

The final category of iPad DAW apps are those that include recording audio tracks as well as synth and sampling. This section includes GarageBand, Music Studio, Meteor Multitrack Recorder, AmpliTube for iPad, and Cubasis.

GarageBand
(free/in-app purchase for software instruments and effects: $4.99)
https://itunes.apple.com/us/app/garageband/id408709785?mt=8

GarageBand on the iPad is the Swiss army knife of music production. It is one of the most complete DAW apps available and an excellent place to start. The app is free to download but requires an in-app purchase of $4.99 to get access to the software instruments and effects. In addition to handling MIDI data and prerecorded loops, it can record audio from external sources, such as vocals and guitars, and internal sources, such as the built-in iPad mic and software synths. It is also compatible with Inter-App Audio and Audiobus, so you can combine other apps (as mentioned earlier in this chapter), greatly expanding the sonic options beyond GarageBand's internal instruments.

GarageBand on the iPad is quite a bit different from the Mac version of the program. There are track limitations, as the iPad version can only record up to eight tracks. However, one of the features that the iPad version offers is Smart Instruments, where you can create automated chords and harmony to a track. See chapter 3 of the book *Musical iPad* for more in-depth information on this feature. If you use the Mac version of GarageBand, you will like the easy way you can share files so you can work on a project on your computer or iPad.

Figure 7.19 GarageBand and Apogee One.

VIDEO 7.8. GARAGEBAND DEMO AND INTER-APP AUDIO.

Figure 7.20
http://youtu.be/j0Q6eJK-pBg

> **Tip:** AmpliTube for iPad was discussed in detail in chapter 3 because of the many options it has for guitar input and processing. In addition to these features, you can also purchase their Premium Recorder as an in-app purchase ($14.99), which turns the built-in one-track recorder to an eight-track audio studio with master effects. It is Inter-App Audio and Audiobus compatible; this can make Amplitude an option for limited multitrack audio recording, in addition to the many other features the app offers (see chapter 3). So if you are already using Amplitude, the recording option can be a consideration to turn the app into a DAW.

Music Studio Lite by Alexander Gross (free)
https://itunes.apple.com/us/app/music-studio-lite/id378356692?mt=8

Music Studio by Alexander Gross ($14.99/in-app purchases available for additional sounds)
https://itunes.apple.com/US/app/id328608539?mt=8

Music Studio cost $10 more than GarageBand, and you get what you pay for in this instance, as there are many more features and high-quality sounds included. There is an excellent-sounding library of instruments that you can use with the virtual keyboard or a MIDI keyboard (see chapter 2), and you can buy additional sounds via in-app purchase. In addition, there is hearty audio track support, making this a complete DAW option. For more information, go to www.xewton.com/musicstudio /features/.

You can download the Lite version to see if you like the interface, and there is a lot you can do in the free version while you make up your mind whether you want to purchase the full version for $14.99.

Figure 7.21 Music Studio.

VIDEO 7.9 MUSIC STUDIO AND LINE 6 MOBILE KEYS.

Figure 7.22
http://youtu.be/6_MEWUrr4AY

Meteor Multitrack Recorder by 4Pockets.com ($19.99/in-app purchases available for additional tracks, sounds, video import, and more)
https://itunes.apple.com/us/app/meteor-multitrack-recorder/id417726727?mt=8

This is a powerful app with Inter-App Audio and Audiobus support. It can record up to 16 tracks and an additional 24 tracks via in-app purchase. Meteor has an impressive feature list and is on a par with other top iPad DAW apps such as Cubasis, reviewed later in this chapter. It can record audio and MIDI and comes with some excellent-sounding instrument samples. If you are still trying to decide on your first fully featured iPad DAW, Meteor is a worthy contender. There are some interesting in-app purchases, such as score to video, so you can include this feature if needed. For more information, check out the review of the app at www.musicappblog.com/music-app -review-meteor/.

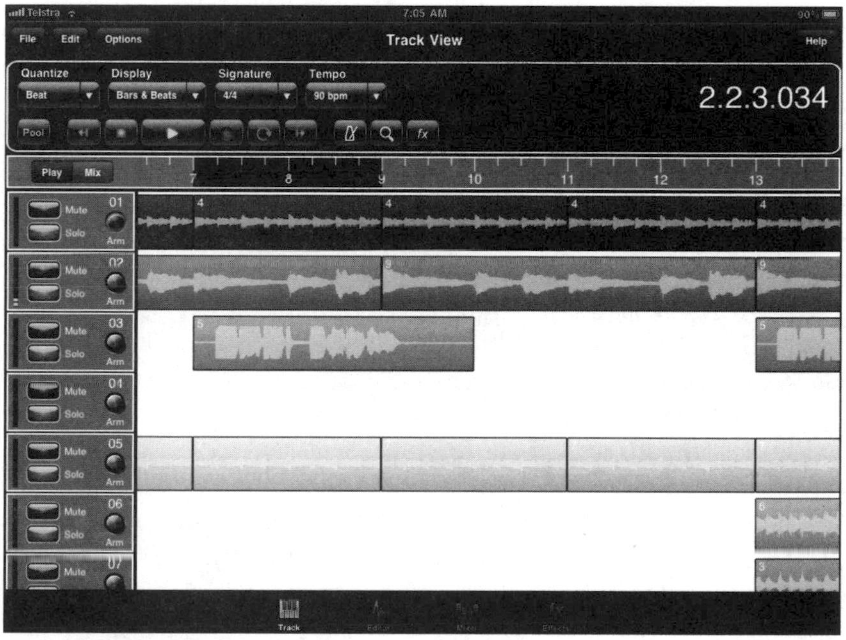

Figure 7.23. Meteor Multitrack Recorder.

VIDEO 7.10 METEOR DEMO.

Figure 7.24
http://youtu.be/vocfH79ID38

> **Tip:** Using Inter-App Audio or Audiobus, you can combine effects and other app sounds with your multitrack DAW. This can enable you to enhance the mixing and mastering of your tracks beyond what is built into the specific iPad DAW app.

Cubasis by Steinberg Media Technologies ($49.99)
https://itunes.apple.com/us/app/cubasis-music-production-system/id583976519?mt=8

The cost of Cubasis ($49.99) may seem astronomical when compared to other DAW apps; however, the price includes all features. There are no in-app purchases to worry about and budget for. Even though $49.99 is a steep price for an iPad DAW app, it is relatively modest when compared to Mac and PC DAWs with the same power. Cubasis is inspired by Steinberg's Cubase DAW for Mac and PC computers. It is a robust and capable multitrack audio and MIDI sequencer.

If you are familiar with Cubase on the Mac or PC, you will notice a similar look and feel; however, Cubasis takes advantage of the iPad's features as well. Projects can consist of both audio and MIDI tracks, and Steinberg mentions that you can create an unlimited number of tracks depending on the memory and power of your iPad (see chapter 1). You can record on multiple tracks at the same time with the appropriate audio interface (see chapters 5 and 6).

For MIDI, there are more than 70 virtual instruments based on their Halion Sonic architecture: www.steinberg.net/en/products/vst/halion_and_halion_sonic/halion_sonic_2.html. These sounds are adequate for most common recording needs. Cubasis has Core MIDI support so you can connect other apps or MIDI devices that you have connected to your iPad (see chapter 2). If you want to experiment with loops, there are over 300 audio and MIDI loops that you can access. The downside is that the current version of the loops does not automatically change to the project's tempo, as is the case with other less expensive apps such as GarageBand.

The built-in effects include reverb, chorus, delay, compression, and EQ. And you can use Inter-App Audio or Audiobus to connect other effects as needed. For more information, check out the specs for Cubasis at www.steinberg.net/en/products/mobile_apps/cubasis.html.

> **Tip:** No matter which DAW iPad app you are using, as long as it supports Inter-App Audio and Audiobus (as all of the apps in this chapter do) or Core MIDI, you can use stand-alone apps for added features. One such app is AudioReverb ($4.99): https://itunes.apple.com/us/app/audioreverb/id670248970?mt=8, a professional reverb plugin.

VIDEO 7.11 AUDIOREVERB DEMO.

Figure 7.25
http://youtu.be/BLTvVs6A0xl

Monitoring Headphones

When recording, headphones are an important part of the studio gear. Using headphones that don't spill sound into the mic while recording is key.

Sennheiser HD 201 Headphones ($29.95)

http://en-us.sennheiser.com/over-ear-headphones-hd-201

The Sennheiser HD 201 is a quality headphone at an affordable price. They are closed-back headphones for increased bass response and comfort. The closed-back, circumaural design helps prevent leakage into your mic when you're recording in your studio, and also helps reject outside noise.

Figure 7.26. Sennheiser HD 201 headphones.

Direct Sound EX-29—Isolating Headphones ($129)

www.extremeheadphones.com/products/ex-29-headphones

The EX-29 closed-back headphones are designed expressly to isolate sound. Their ear cushions are comfortable for the listener, yet they act as a superb barrier between the headphones' speakers and your live microphones. You don't have to worry about bleed from the headphones being recorded during a take. They are ideal for recording in the studio, and they can be used when you are mixing and mastering your tracks, as they are designed for high-fidelity performance. The EX-29 is also designed for comfort, so you can wear them for long periods of time. A padded and adjustable headband lets you position them in the best location, while heavily padded ear cushions cup over your ear, creating a closed-back chamber of sound. And the EX-29's long nine-foot cable lets you get ready to perform and monitor virtually anywhere in the studio. The EX-29s save time in the studio with their innovative "Red is Right" feature: the inside ear panel of the right channel is covered with bright red fabric. The EX-29 comes with both a 1/4-inch and a 1/8-inch jack.

Figure 7.27. EX-29 headphones.

Powered Studio Monitors

There are two options when considering monitors for your recording studio: active and passive. Passive monitors require an amplifier, and active speakers have the power built into the cabinet that houses the speaker. This makes them portable and easy to use with the output of your iPad. Included in this section are just two of the many options for quality studio monitors. If you are looking for live performance speakers, see chapter 4.

Behringer MS16 Active Monitor ($119.99 list price per pair)
www.behringer.com/EN/Products/MS16.aspx

The Behringer MS16 is a compact two-way stereo speaker system for the home studio. Eight watts drive the MS16's 4-inch woofer and high-resolution tweeter. There are controls on the front of each speaker for volume, bass, and treble. There are two stereo line inputs (RCA and 1/8 TRS), so you can connect up to two stereo sources or devices—for example, the output of your iPad and an audio or instrument source. There is also a mixer option, so you can plug in a microphone and mix its volume with the other input. Magnetic shielding and compact size make the Behringer MS16 ideal for placement near video monitors or computer displays.

Figure 7.28 Behringer MS16 Active Monitor.

JBL LSR305 5" Active Studio Monitor ($199.99 list price for one monitor)
www.jblpro.com/www/products/recording-broadcast/3-series#.U3OSPC-_K30

JBL LSR305 active studio monitors are designed for the serious audio engineer or music producer. They're great for mixing music in your DAW software, editing video, or any other task that requires precise, accurate, detailed sound. JBL designed the LSR305 with advanced features and has even earned the acclaim of renowned engineer Frank Filipetti. An innovative Image Control Waveguide creates a well-defined and incredibly dimensional stereo image.

Figure 7.29. JBL LSR305 5" Active Studio Monitor.

Genelec 8020C Active Monitor ($595 list price per speaker)

www.genelec.com/products/8020c/

The small Genelec 8020C has been designed for monitoring in difficult listening environments, particularly those compromised by lack of space, making this an ideal speaker for the home or professional studio. It is compact and includes a cast-aluminum enclosure and a 4-inch LF driver and 3/4-inch tweeter with dual 20-watt amplifiers. With the addition an Iso-Pod stand, the Genelec 8020C can also be stand or wall mounted.

Figure 7.30 Genelec 8020C.

Speaker Placement App

For studio engineers, speaker setup and placement is extremely important. It can mean the difference in a quality mix.

SpeakerAngle by AudioAppsStore ($0.99)
https://itunes.apple.com/us/app/speakerangle/id549033688?mt=8

Genelec has developed an app to aid you in the process of properly placing your speakers in your studio. SpeakerAngle for iPad assists you with monitor and surround sound setups for optimal performance. SpeakerAngle works by setting your iPad on top of your speakers. You set the speaker so that it is facing straight ahead, and then the app guides you within industry recommendations—eventually getting your speakers matched in angling. This app is especially effective if you work in different locations.

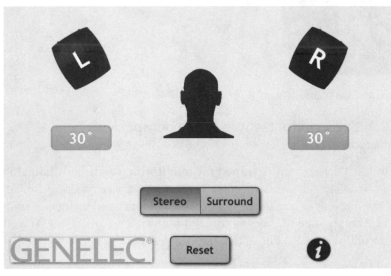

Figure 7.31 SpeakerAngle.

File Sharing and Management

Audio and DAW files can be quite large, and the memory on your iPad can get filled up quickly. Therefore, you should consider a way to export and store your files in places other than the iPad itself.

In chapter 1, the basics of file sharing was introduced—namely, connecting your iPad to your computer and using iTunes to move files back and forth. For more information on iOS file sharing, go to http://support.apple.com/kb/ht4094.

Dropbox Paid Options

Also in chapter 1, using Dropbox for file storage was mentioned. Many of the DAW apps in this chapter support saving your files to Dropbox. Many apps support Dropbox, including Cubasis, Auria, Beatmaker 2, Music Studio, and more. For a list of file types currently supported by Dropbox, go to https://www.dropbox.com/help/80/en. You can access your Dropbox files directly via the iPad app.

Dropbox (Free)
https://itunes.apple.com/us/app/dropbox/id327630330?mt=8

For DAW recording, consider purchasing additional space from Dropbox, beyond the amount they offer for free. The Pro upgrade includes a total of 100 GB of storage, and the Business option features unlimited space. Go to www.dropbox.com/pricing to review the cost and options for the Dropbox Pro account.

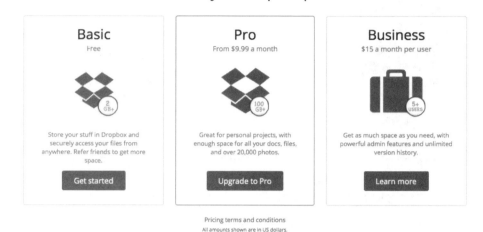

Figure 7.32 Dropbox plans.

SoundCloud (free)

https://itunes.apple.com/us/app/soundcloud/id336353151?mt=8

SoundCloud Pro service is available for a $5 monthly subscription fee, which includes up to four total hours of recording time; Pro Unlimited costs $15 monthly, which includes unlimited storage space. With a paid subscription, you can spotlight certain tracks and have them appear at the top of your profile. You'll also have access to data and feedback on your listeners: who they are and if they are downloading and/or embedding your files. And you can choose to show or hide comments or stats.

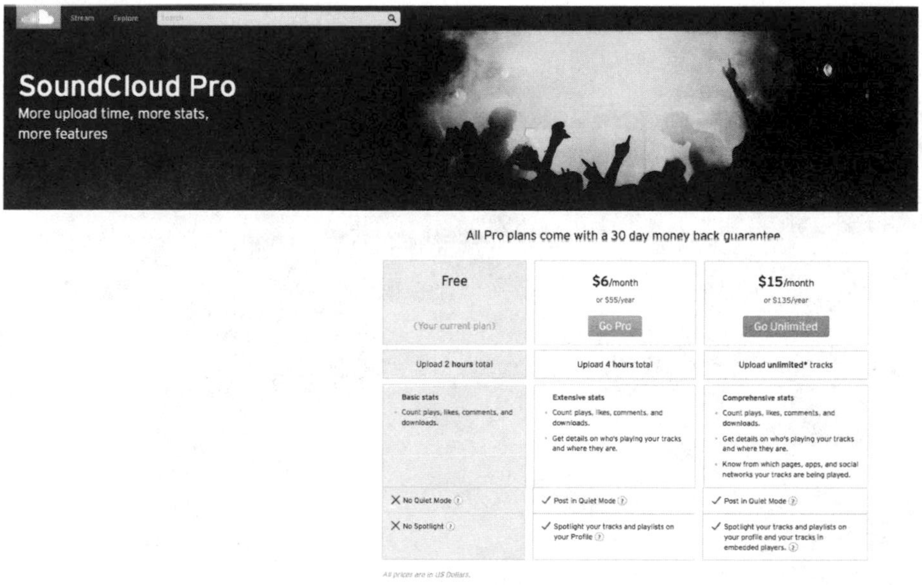

All Pro plans come with a 30 day money back guarantee.

Free	$6/month	$15/month
	or $55/year	or $135/year
(Your current plan)	Go Pro	Go Unlimited
Upload 2 hours total	Upload 4 hours total	Upload unlimited* tracks
Basic stats	Extensive stats	Comprehensive stats
· Count plays, likes, comments, and downloads.	· Count plays, likes, comments, and downloads.	· Count plays, likes, comments, and downloads.
	· Get details on who's playing your tracks and where they are.	· Get details on who's playing your tracks and where they are.
		· Know from which pages, apps, and social networks your tracks are being played.
✗ No Quiet Mode	✓ Post in Quiet Mode	✓ Post in Quiet Mode
✗ No Spotlight	✓ Spotlight your tracks and playlists on your Profile	✓ Spotlight your tracks and playlists on your profile and your tracks in embedded players.

All prices are in US Dollars.

Figure 7.33 SoundCloud Pro.

VIDEO 7.12 SOUNDCLOUD PRO AND UNLIMITED DEMO.

Figure 7.34
http://youtu.be/zSit5DHq_Jc

AudioShare—Audio Document Manager by Kymatica (Jonatan Liljedahl) ($3.99)

https://itunes.apple.com/us/app/audioshare-audio-document/id543859300?mt=8

AudioShare is an audio document manager for the iPad with powerful import and export abilities. You can organize your audio or sound files on your device using folders, which can be arranged according to your personal preference. You can also transfer sound files between apps and between the iPad and your computer. For example, you can take a sound file from Dropbox and share it on SoundCloud. Or audiocopy sounds from your favorite music-making app and import them into the AudioShare library, for later sharing or copying into other apps. Or use the built-in web browser to download sound files directly from the Internet. Some apps have a dedicated "Export to AudioShare" button. AudioShare supports all sound file formats, bit depths, and rates that have built-in support in iOS: AIFF, AIFC, WAVE, SoundDesigner2, Next, MP3, MP2, MP1, AC3, AAC_ADTS, MPEG4, M4A, CAF, 3GP, 3GP2, and AMR.

You can record directly in AudioShare, from interfaces (see chapter 6), Inter-App Audio, or other Audiobus compatible apps. You can also preview and play sound files with waveform display and looping, trim and normalize sound files, and convert to other file formats.

Figure 7.35. AudioShare.

VIDEO 7.13 AUDIOSHARE TO DROPBOX DEMO.

Figure 7.36
http://youtu.be/G6nbZ3J2HjQ

Multitrack Studio Options

The following are four sample studio options at a low, moderate, and high cost.

Multitrack Studio Option 1 (low to moderate cost):

One iPad, DAW and related apps, monitoring headphones, powered studio monitors, file storage, microphone, and audio interface.

- iPad (additional memory capacity will increase the price; check the Apple site for more details: www.apple.com/ipad/compare/): $499.00–$599.00
- DAW app: $4.99–$19.99
- Additional apps (AudioShare and SpeakerAngle): $5.99
- Monitoring headphones: $29.95
- Powered studio monitors (per pair): $119.95
- File storage (annual cost): no cost–$119.88
- Microphone (see chapter 5): $39.99
- Audio interface (see chapter 6): $39.99–$49.99

Total cost: $734.91–983.98

Multitrack Studio Option 2 (moderate cost):

One iPad with additional memory, DAW and related apps, monitoring headphones, powered studio monitors, file storage, microphone, and audio interface.

- iPad (additional memory capacity will increase the price; check the Apple site for more details: www.apple.com/ipad/compare/): $599.00–$699.00
- DAW app: $10.00–$40.00
- Additional apps: (AudioShare and SpeakerAngle): $5.99
- Monitoring headphones: $29.95
- Powered studio monitors (per pair): $119.95–$399.98
- File storage (annual cost): $119.88
- Microphone (see chapter 5): $99.99
- Audio Interface (see chapter 6): $59.99–$119.99

Total cost: $1,053.98–$1,524.77

Multitrack Studio Option 3 (high cost):

One iPad with additional memory, DAW and related apps, monitoring headphones, powered studio monitors, file storage, microphone, and audio interface.

- iPad (additional memory capacity will increase the price; check the Apple site for more details: www.apple.com/ipad/compare/): $699.00–$799.00

- DAW app: $19.99–$49.99
- Additional apps (AudioShare and SpeakerAngle): $5.99
- Monitoring headphones: $129.00
- Powered studio monitors (per pair): $399.98–$1,190.00
- file storage (unlimited) (annual cost): $180.00
- Microphone (see chapter 5): $299.99
- Audio interface (see chapter 6): $119.99–$1,395.99

Total cost: $1,852.95–$4,047.98

Chapter 7 Activities

1. Download GarageBand or another DAW app, and experiment with recording using all of the options: audio, loops, and MIDI.
2. Download both GarageBand and Music Studio Lite, as both are free. Compare their features, interfaces, and options.
3. Using Audiobus or Inter-App Audio, record from an app into your DAW program. Be sure that the DAW you are using is compatible with Audiobus or Inter-App Audio.
4. Create a free Dropbox account, and send/save a sound file created in your DAW.
5. Create a free SoundCloud account, and upload a sound file created in your DAW.
6. Select one of the multitrack studio options, and make adjustments to suit your needs.

Summary

In this chapter, we looked a variety of iPad apps for multitrack recording, editing, and mastering, making the iPad the center of your music studio. The chapter also addressed Audiobus and Inter-App technology, which allows you to record and apply effects across apps. Monitoring headphones and powered studio monitors were also covered, along with file storage options, including Dropbox and SoundCloud.

Chapter **8**

THE iPad WITH COMPUTERS AND MIXERS

This chapter addresses the many iPad applications in the music studio and performance. The iPad can communicate with computers, mixers, and digital audio recorders, either by direct connection or wirelessly over Bluetooth and Wi-Fi. It can send and receive messages using MIDI and OSC (Open Sound Control), and with the appropriate apps, it can add features and functionality to hardware interfaces, mixers, and computer software.

Connecting iPads Using Bluetooth or WiFi

The iPad can connect wirelessly to other iPads, and there are a few apps that take advantage of this to provide different performance options. Four performers, each with his or her own iPad, can play together using GarageBand's Jam feature (this is mentioned in the *Musical iPad*, chapter 5 [page 105]). The iPads communicate over Bluetooth to record the jam, and all four recordings are transferred to the master iPad at the end of the performance.

VIDEO 8.1. GARAGEBAND JAM.

Figure 8.1
http://youtu.be/1aJxCgVkFS0

WIST

Korg developed a way to use two iPads together, through a technology called WIST (Wireless Sync Start Technology). WIST uses Bluetooth to connect the iPads. Once WIST is activated in both apps, the first app to start will assume the role of master, and the other iPad will sync to it when you start and stop playback. Look for WIST compatibility in the app descriptions on the iTunes store, or go to the WIST website to view a list of compatible apps: www.korguser.net/wist/.

Figure 8.2. WIST activation on iMini.

VIDEO 8.2. WIST DEMO.

Figure 8.3
http://youtu.be/bTZ0KWBci9E

Apollo MIDI over Bluetooth by Secret Base Design ($4.99)
https://itunes.apple.com/us/app/apollo-midi-over-bluetooth/id720942905?mt=8

Apollo MIDI over Bluetooth uses Bluetooth LE (low energy) to send MIDI data to another iPad or a Mac computer. PC computers are not supported. This app requires an iPad 3 or later, the iPad Mini, or the iPhone 4S or later, as these support Bluetooth LE. The computer must also be a recent model, with Bluetooth LE or a USB Bluetooth adapter installed. The Apollo for OSX software is available for free in the Mac App Store.

The app has an A Endpoint and a B Endpoint button. Select one device as the A endpoint and the other as the B endpoint, then press Search on both devices, and they should detect each other. The connection is bidirectional, so MIDI can be sent from either device to the other.

Figure 8.4. Apollo MIDI over Bluetooth.

VIDEO 8.3. APOLLO MIDI OVER BLUETOOTH FOR IOS AND OSX.

Figure 8.5
http://youtu.be/tuwvnkNKvyk

Connecting to MIDI Hardware

Chapter 2 dealt with connecting the iPad to a single MIDI keyboard. This section deals with connecting two or more devices via MIDI to the iPad. Using this type of hardware, the iPad can function as the sound source connected to a computer, or as the principal DAW, as described in chapter 7.

iConnectMIDI2+ by iConnectivity ($99.99)
www.iconnectivity.com/iConnectMIDI2plus

iConnectivity offers two hardware options that connect the iPad to simple and complex MIDI rigs. The first is iConnectivity2+, a hardware MIDI interface that can accommodate two computing devices, a computer or iPad, and two 5-pin DIN MIDI devices. The unit connects directly to the iPad via a provided USB to 30-pin cable. The 30-pin to Lightning adapter is supported by newer iPads. On the front panel, there are two USB device ports for connecting an iPad and a computer. Port 1 supports both MIDI and Audio passThru™. Audio passThru™ is iConnectivity's feature that allows audio files to be digitally transmitted between an iPad and a Mac or PC computer. The back panel has two 5-pin MIDI DIN connectors, so you can connect up to two MIDI devices. iConnectMIDI2+ supports 10 ports of 16 channels of MIDI I/O per port.

When using iConnectMIDI2+, if you want to charge the iPad while it is connected, you must purchase the iConnectMIDI2+ Optional Power Transformer ($29.99).

Figure 8.6. iConnectMIDI2+.

VIDEO 8.4. ICONNECTMIDI2+ TOUR.

Figure 8.7A
http://youtu.be/PHnP6G6IVRw

iConnectMIDI4+ by iConnectivity ($249.99)
www.iconnectivity.com/iConnectMIDI4plus

iConnectMIDI4+ is a hardware interface that can handle large, complex MIDI setups. Just like the iConnectMIDI2+, it is USB class compliant, so it can plug into the iPad via the Apple Camera Connector Kit. It has three USB device ports for connecting iOS devices and/or Mac or PC computers. The iConnectMIDI4+ has Audio passThru™ technology, so audio files can be digitally transferred between all three device ports. There are four sets of five-pin DIN MIDI connectors, accommodating up to four MIDI devices. For USB MIDI devices, there is a USB MIDI host port for a single device, or you can use a USB hub to connect up to eight devices. There is also an Ethernet port for connecting a wireless router, enabling iOS devices and computers to link wirelessly to the iConnectMIDI4+. iConnectMIDI4+ supports 64 ports of 16-channel MIDI I/O per port.

Figure 8.7B. iConnectMIDI4+.

Sample Players and Synthesizers

The iPad can be used in several different capacities with hardware and software synthesizers and sample players. From the studio to the stage to sound design, the iPad can add function and control to hardware and computer software synths and sampler players.

Roland Patch Editors

Roland has free patch editing apps for several models of their hardware synthesizers. To work wirelessly, these apps require the Roland WNA1100-RL Wireless USB Adapter ($52.99 list price). If you don't have the USB adapter, the iPad can be connected to the device using a USB cable and the Apple Camera Connection Kit. The apps provide a larger screen interface than those available on a keyboard synth. For synth modules like the Integra-7, it may be more convenient to have the iPad at arm's length than the instrument's front panel. Check out the Roland Wireless Connect website for an up-to-date list of apps and supported hardware: www.roland.com /products/WirelessConnect/.

JP Synth Editor by Roland Systems Group (free)

https://itunes.apple.com/us/app/jp-synth-editor/id521977766?mt–8

JP Synth Editor is a patch editor for Roland Jupiter-80 and Jupiter-50 synthesizers. The app can edit existing sounds or create new ones. All of the synth's parameters fit on the iPad's screen. Any change made on the iPad is instantly transferred to the synth. Jupiter Synths use a combination of sampled and synthesized sounds. Only the synthesized sounds can be edited. Saving edited and new sounds must be done using the synthesizer's controls, as the app cannot save sounds.

Figure 8.08. JP Synth Editor.

VIDEO 8.5. JUPITER80/JUPITER50 SYNTH EDITOR FOR IPAD.

Figure 8.09
http://youtu.be/vPxftoHksOo

Integra-7 Editor by Roland Systems Group (free)
https://itunes.apple.com/us/app/integra-7-editor/id551547016?mt=8

The Integra-7 synth module contains a collection of 6,000 sounds. It features a mixer and multiple effects, including Roland's Motional Surround, allowing you to place sounds in a 360-degree sound field. The Integra-7 Editor for the iPad offers a large graphic touch screen interface that is much easier to use than the front panel of any synth. The mixer page allows you to control the output level of each sound in a multitimbral setup. The mixer has panning controls, a mute button, and a three-band EQ. It can accommodate 16 individual instruments and uses a horizontal swipe gesture to move between the left and right sides of the virtual mixing board.

The Tone page takes the 16 available tracks and displays them in horizontal strips. You can easily select tones for each track and view the Levels, Panning, and Effects settings on the Mixer page.

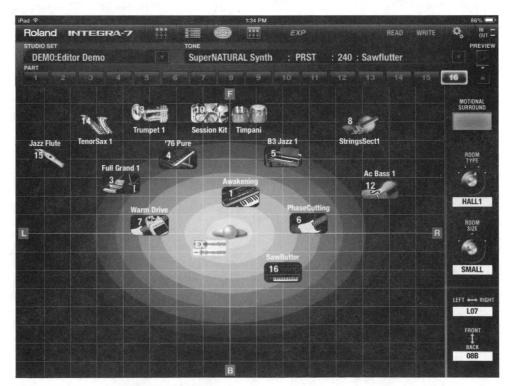

Figure 8.10. Integra-7 Motional Surround page.

The Motional Surround page displays each tone loaded into the 16 available channels as an icon over a grid. The top-to-bottom axis controls front-to-back placement, and the left-to-right axis is stereo left and right. Each instrument can be manually positioned on the three-dimensional grid. Controls for the type and size of the reverb effect applied to each instrument are displayed on the right side of the screen.

The synth editor page allows editing of the synthesized sounds in the Integra-7. All changes are communicated to the module instantly, but saving any changes must be done on the Integra-7 itself.

VIDEO 8.6. INTEGRA-7 EDITOR.

Figure 8.11
http://youtu.be/y_yNd0B823k

Omni TR by Spectrasonics (free)
https://itunes.apple.com/us/app/omni-tr/id414496008?mt=8

Omni TR turns the iPad into a performance-oriented remote control surface for Spectrasonics Omnisphere, a software synthesizer for Mac and Windows computers. Omni TR requires iOS 4.2 or later, and Omnisphere 1.5.1 or later. PC users must install Apple's Bonjour.

Omni TR has four pages of real-time control. You can build a combination of up to eight sounds. The Main page is where sounds are selected. The mix can be controlled from the right side of the screen, using the volume sliders and the mute and solo buttons. Each part can be latched individually (the notes played are frozen and will repeat until changed), and Trigger mode allows for parts to be synchronized and quantized in real-time performance.

The Orb TR is a circular controller that is available on the computer screen, but it takes on a new dimension when used with the iPad's touch screen interface. The Orb page allows intelligent modification of an Omnisphere sound in real time by dragging your finger around the circular control area on the screen. Click the Dice button for the app to "roll the dice" and create its own variations. The Depth slider controls the depth of the effect. It is possible to record your, or the app's, movements and save them as a part of the patch.

The Controls page has a pitch ribbon for bending pitches, and a mixer-like section where the selected sound's parameters are displayed and can be remixed to create variations on the sound. The Jumbo page is for live performance. It displays the loaded sounds from the Main page in large buttons that are more visible in concert lighting.

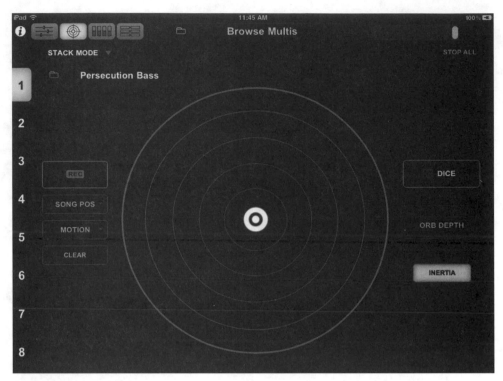

Figure 8.12. Omni TR Orb page.

VIDEO 8.7. OMNI TR DEMO.

Figure 8.13
http://youtu.be/yds-JU_EHZc

VI PRO Remote by Vienna Instruments
(free with software purchase from www.vsl.com)
www.vsl.co.at/en/211/497/537/1456/2533/2181.htm

VI PRO Remote is a real-time wireless remote controller for use with Vienna Instruments PRO orchestra samples running on a Mac or PC computer. The app creates a two-way connection with Vienna Instruments PRO running on a computer-based DAW. Changes made on one device are automatically updated on the other. Use the app for switching between instrument articulations, or fader movements such as Master Volume, Velocity Crossfade, Expression, and Tuning. All actions can be recorded in a DAW as MIDI data for future playback and recording. VI PRO Remote also works with Vienna Instruments PRO's internal APP Sequencer. Switch between chord inversions, scales, root keys of scales, and instrument articulations. The iPad must be running iOS 5.1 or later.

Figure 8.14. VI Pro Remote.

VIDEO 8.8. VI PRO REMOTE DEMO.

Figure 8.15
http://youtu.be/CuLg8z3sLXl

Software DAWs

There are many apps that offer wireless control over computer-based software DAWs (iPad DAWs were addressed in chapter 7). Prices vary, from free software-specific controllers to more expensive apps with larger feature sets and the ability to work with DAWs from different software companies on both Mac and Windows computers. Third-party apps (apps made by different companies than the software they control) usually require a few more steps to configure. Look for the documentation and tutorials online for the proper procedures to link up your devices and software. Carefully read the app's page in iTunes, and make sure your computer software version is supported. Also, read the reviews to learn what other users of the app are experiencing.

Single DAW Apps

The apps listed in this section work with a single computer-based DAW software program.

touchAble by AppBC ($24.99)

https://itunes.apple.com/us/app/touchable/id385949475?mt=8

touchAble turns the iPad into a controller for the computer software program Ableton Live, available for Mac and PC computers. Connection between the iPad and the computer is over Wi-Fi. In addition to the app on your iPad, you will need to download and install a driver from the app developer's website onto your computer.

touchAble uses an icon-driven, modular interface that can show either a single module in full-screen display or a top and bottom split with two modules on the screen. Modules include Clips, Mixer, Devices, Keys and Pads, XY Pad, Template Editor, and, for Live 9 users, Browser. If you need more onscreen controls than is possible on a single iPad, a second iPad can be linked to the same Ableton Live session. This allows you to tweak the mixer faders on one iPad while playing a virtual synth—inside Ableton Live—on the second iPad screen. As long as the second iPad is synced with the iTunes account used to purchase the first copy, you will not need to purchase a second copy of the app.

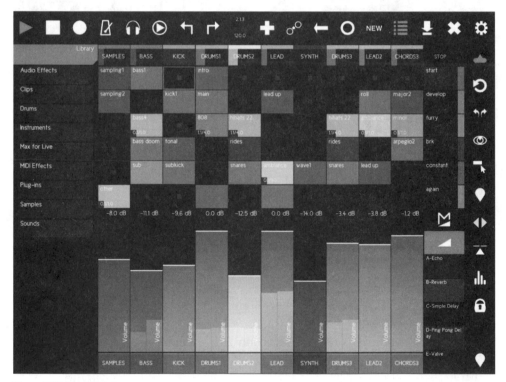

Figure 8.16. touchAble 2.

VIDEO 8.9. TOUCHABLE 2.

Figure 8.17
http://youtu.be/zmHhJ-G-Yfc

Cubase iC Pro by Steinberg ($16.99)

https://itunes.apple.com/us/app/cubase-ic-pro/id573140262?mt=8

Cubase iC Pro is designed to be a remote extension for Cubase software running on a Mac or PC computer. It requires a free driver to be installed on your computer so that the computer version will recognize the iPad app as a controller. Communication is over a Wi-Fi network. Once connected, any changes you make to a project on your computer will automatically be updated on the iPad. Cubase iC Pro is compatible with Cubase versions 6.5 and later, Cubase Artist versions 6.5 and later, and Cubase LE AI Elements 6 and 7. Some functions only work with Cubase 6.5 and later, so check the app's iTunes page for the latest news on compatibility. The Project page provides a project overview. The transport controls are located at the bottom of the screen. You can use pinch and spread gestures to zoom in and out of your tracks. One of the key features of the Mix Console page is the ability to create up to four independent monitor mixes when recording. The Key Commands page allows you to create custom sets of commands and macros that can be accessed with a single touch of a button on the iPad screen. The app offers split-screen modes so you can combine page views.

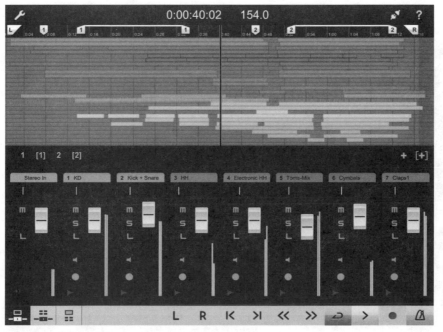

Figure 8.18. Cubase iC Pro.

VIDEO 8.10. CUBASE IC PRO DEMO.

Figure 8.19
http://youtu.be/ws9pV30Vfy8

Tip: There is a free version of the Cubase iC Pro app called Cubase iC. It is available for the iPhone and allows wireless control of the transport function, monitoring the playback position, and controlling the Arranger Track in Cubase: https://itunes.apple.com/us/app/cubase-ic/id316698235?mt=8.

Logic Remote by Apple (free)
https://itunes.apple.com/us/app/logic-remote/id638394624?mt=8

Logic Remote is a companion app for Logic X on the Mac. If you don't own Logic X but do own Apple's GarageBand 10.0 or MainStage 3.0.2 software, Logic Remote works with those software packages as well. The app connects over Wi-Fi to the Mac. Both the iPad and computer must be on the same network.

Logic Remote is able to access the help documentation for Logic Pro X, MainStage 3, and GarageBand on the Mac. The Mixer page offers control for Logic's faders, including the ability to move multiple faders at a time. A bar ruler of all tracks appears at the top of the page. Swipe the ruler area to navigate to any location in your session. You can operate the basic transport controls from anywhere in your studio with a single touch.

Figure 8.20. Logic Remote.

Multitouch gestures can be used for volume, pan, solo, and mute controls. Use care when touching the screen on the Mixer page, as you can easily move a fader level when swiping. The app has pages for playing and editing software instruments. The Key Commands page allows you to use preset buttons for functions in Logic and create your own custom set. Use key commands to run Logic from anywhere in your studio.

VIDEO 8.11. LOGIC REMOTE DEMO.

Figure 8.21
http://youtu.be/VVokdEWOqX0

DP Control by MOTU Inc. (free)
https://itunes.apple.com/us/app/dp-control/id380483770?mt=8

DP Control turns the iPad into a mobile control surface for Digital Performer, a software DAW that runs on Mac and Windows computers. The app requires Digital Performer 7.2 or higher. Communication between the iPad and the computer is over a Wi-Fi network, and both the computer and the iPad must be on the same network. This app is perfect for self-recording, allowing you to record your own performances when you can't be physically at the computer to start and stop recording.

The app gives you complete control over Digital Performer's main transport functions, including Play, Rewind, Count Off, and Overdub. The time counter has settings for real time, SMPTE time, samples, and marker names. Marker names can be created and named from DP Control, and you can scroll through them to locate a point in the song to begin recording or playback. For record-enabled tracks, you can create a new take or cycle through existing takes. Takes can be renamed or deleted from the app.

On the Tracks page, you can view a complete list of tracks, including collapsible nested track folders organized exactly as they are on the computer screen. DP Control provides the ability to solo, mute, record-enable, and play or record automation. On the Mixer page, you have control over volume and panning. Since communication goes both ways, any changes you make on the computer are reflected in the app and vice versa. In Settings, you can manage your computer connections, and if your sequence contains multiple chunks, you can select a specific chunk to play. This is helpful for using DP Control with Digital Performer in a live setting for backing tracks or click tracks. Set up a set of sequences as chunks in a set list, and DP Control can be used to switch between chunks.

Figure 8.22. DP Control.

VIDEO 8.12. DP CONTROL DEMO.

Figure 8.23
http://youtu.be/cU3oTsfVTQc

Multiple DAW Apps

There are apps that work with a variety of computer software DAWs. Some allow you to begin work with a minimum of setup between the iPad and computer and have the necessary interface ready to use. Other apps offer the ability to create your own custom controllers in the layout of your choice. The first two apps in this section support a broad range of DAWs and come ready to connect and use. Then, for the more adventurous user, there are two apps where you can create the controller interface that best suits your workflow.

AC-7 Core HD by Saitara Software ($4.99)
https://itunes.apple.com/us/app/ac-7-core-hd/id586159945?mt=8

AC-7 Core HD is a mixer control interface reminiscent of the Mackie Hui hardware controller. The AC-7's interface is the same for each software DAW. The list of compatible DAW software includes Logic Pro, Pro Tools, Digital Performer, Sonar, Ableton Live, Reason, Vegas, PreSonus Studio 1, Tracktion, Audition, and Cubase/Nuendo. The documentation provides setup instructions particular to each DAW.

The app works wirelessly with Mac and PC computers, or with a wired connection using a USB cable and the Apple Camera Connection Kit. For wireless connections, both the iPad and computer must be on the same network.

The app provides transport control, mixer control over levels, panning, mute, solo, and record-enable settings. A Bank button flanked by Forward and Back Arrow keys will navigate through mixer channels in groups of eight. The scribble strip will reflect the information you've typed in for track names in the DAW. Next to the counter at the top of the screen is the Set Up button for choosing your DAW. Once it is selected, the area under the counter will change to two rows of Function buttons. Swipe to the left and right to access the different pages.

AC-7 Core HD is a redesign of the original AC-7 Core app that is still available in the app store. The developer made the choice to keep the old app in the store for customers still using the first-generation iPad. The HD version requires iOS 6, which the original iPad cannot run. The downside is that users of the original app running newer iPads must repurchase it to get the latest features. This is an issue that may become more prevalent as iOS recording moves forward and the older hardware is no longer supported.

Figure 8.24. AC-7 Core HD.

VIDEO 8.13. AC-7 CORE HD DEMO.

Figure 8.25
http://youtu.be/BKVhHGK0ahA

V-Control Pro by Neyrinck ($49.99)
https://itunes.apple.com/us/app/v-control-pro/id400423823?mt=8

V-Control Pro was one of the first apps to offer DAW mixer control on the iPad. It now has an impressive list of supported software applications, including Pro Tools, Logic, Digital Performer, SONAR, Ableton Live, Reason, FL Studio, PreSonus Studio One, Cubase, and Nuendo.

V-Control uses different graphical appearance packages, or *skins*, for each software DAW it supports. The app control begins with a transport, basic mixer functions, sends editing, automation modes, and grouping and ungrouping of tracks, and includes, with the most recent update, a jog shuttle wheel. An edit pop-over window gives you access to additional controls to assist with your work. There are also buttons for Input Monitor, Undo, and Save.

The V-Window feature allows you to display and control plug-in windows on the iPad. You can tweak EQ settings or control a virtual instrument via the iPad touch screen. Since the app is designed for mouse-and-drag operation, the iPad's multitouch gestures are not supported. The complete feature set varies according to the computer software the app is controlling.

Pro Tools users are able to use V-Control along with Ethernet-connected controllers such as D-Command, C24, and Pro Control. Recording engineers who work on a variety of DAWs can use V-Control for a variety of work situations. There are videos available demonstrating each supported DAW on the Neyrinck website (www.neyrinck.com/v -control-pro-support) and YouTube.

Figure 8.26. V-Control Pro.

VIDEO 8.14. V-CONTROL PRO DEMO.

Figure 8.27
http://youtu.be/09ACT1Ez8U0

TouchOSC by Robert FISHER ($4.99)

https://itunes.apple.com/us/app/touchosc/id288120394?mt=8

TouchOSC is a MIDI and OSC (Open Sound Control) control surface app for iPad. Open Sound Control is a content format for messaging between computers, synthesizers, and other multimedia devices optimized for networking. It sends messages using Wi-Fi and via Core MIDI inter app communication to computers running compatible DAW software and hardware. Compatible interfaces include all mark II or mark III interfaces and the 4pre, Track 16, MicroBook, MicroBook II, and PCI-424 core systems. The documentation for TouchOSC is available at http://hexler.net/docs/touchosc.

You can create a template using the iPad app, or download the free TouchOSC Editor software for Mac or Windows computer.

If you own a recent-model MOTU audio interface with Cue Mix FX software included, you can use TouchOSC to wirelessly control the mixer levels. The iPad communicates with the interface via a computer also running Cue Mix FX. The computer version controls the software on the interface.

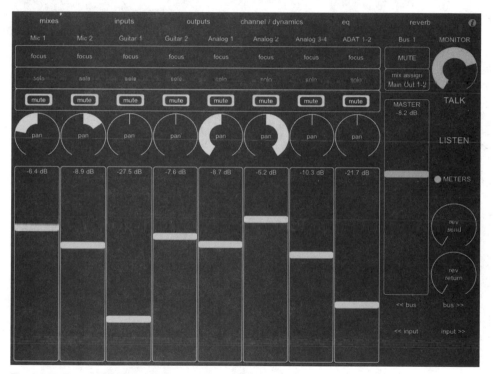

Figure 8.28. TouchOSC MOTU interface template.

VIDEO 8.15. TOUCHOSC WITH ABLETON LIVE DEMO.

Figure 8.29
http://youtu.be/4Fiwz5-neGk

MIDI Designer Pro by Confusionists LLC ($19.99)
https://itunes.apple.com/us/app/midi-designer-pro/id492291712?mt=8

The MIDI Designer iPad app allows you to design custom MIDI controllers for anything that communicates via MIDI. You can connect the iPad to MIDI devices via Wi-Fi, or hardware such as iConnectMIDI2 or Line 6 MIDI Mobilizer II. The Lite version of the app, MIDI Designer Lite by Confusionists LLC, is identical to the Pro version but with a small advertising bar added. The Pro version has no ads.

The Designer 12 version is limited to twelve controls. MIDI Designer has a library of customizable knobs, sliders, XY Pads, and more. Choose the color and texture of the background and LED color. You can create a total of eight banks, each consisting of six pages. A collection of layouts for synthesizers and apps can be found on the Midi Designer website: http://mididesigner.com/community/.

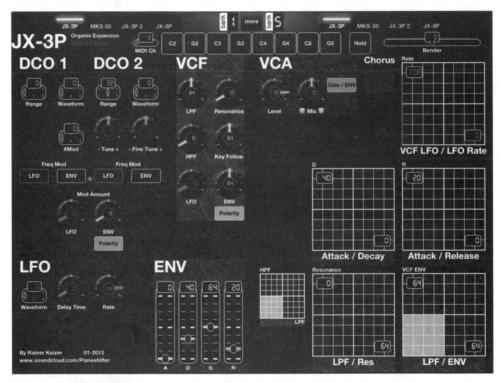

Figure 8.30 MIDI Designer Pro.

VIDEO 8.16. MIDI DESIGNER PRO DEMO.

Figure 8.31
http://youtu.be/rwMjOTjzTS8

Lemur by Liine ($24.99)

https://itunes.apple.com/us/app/lemur/id481290621?mt=8

Lemur began as a multitouch screen MIDI controller for sequencers, synthesizers, and virtual instruments. It has been repackaged for the iPad as a MIDI and OSC (Open Sound Control) controller. You can create custom faders, buttons, knobs, and menus. They are assembled into custom templates and configured to send MIDI or OSC commands to software on your computer such as Ableton Live, Reaktor, Traktor, Modul8, and others.

Lemur interfaces can be programmed directly on the app or by using the Lemur Editor software on a computer. The Editor software is a free download from the Liine website: https://liine.net/en/support/lemur. User guides and tutorial videos for the computer editor and the iPad app are available on the site support page.

The in-app editor has a list of objects that can be displayed on the screen. You then assign MIDI or OSC (Open Sound Control) messages and edit scripts using multitouch menus. Lemur supports MIDI interfaces such as iRig and iConnect MIDI and can address up to eight simultaneous MIDI or OSC devices.

Lemur is a popular controller for Ableton Live Mac and PC versions using both the Live Control 2 template and custom-designed templates. The Lemur website has a user library where you can download templates created by other users.

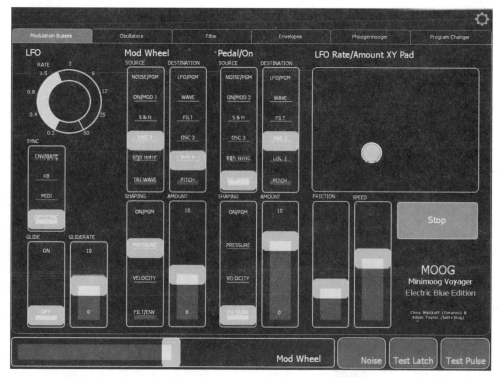

Figure 8.32. A Lemur-created Synthesizer Control page.

VIDEO 8.17. LEMUR DEMO.

Figure 8.33
http://youtu.be/ouTLi5SmMuw

Figure 8.34. Live Control 2.

VIDEO 8.18. LIVE CONTROL 2 DEMO.

Figure 8.35.
http://youtu.be/13LhO-g7Ki0

Tip: With any third-party product, there may be times when a software update to the DAW or iOS causes compatibility issues. I advise waiting for a short period before updating any software, as issues are typically identified and resolved. Check the app developer's website and blogs for information on compatibility. *Never* upgrade software while you are mid-project!

Keypad Controllers

Keypad apps offer wireless remote control capability but limit control functions to keystroke commands.

Custom Keypad by Out of Web Site! ($3.99)

https://itunes.apple.com/us/app/custom-keypad/id433683617?mt=8

Custom Keypad can create application-specific keypad layouts for computer software. Custom Keypad works with Mac, PC, and Linux computers and any computer application that supports VNC (Virtual Network Computing). To create a keypad, use the button types provided in the app, define their function, and then connect to your computer to test and use.

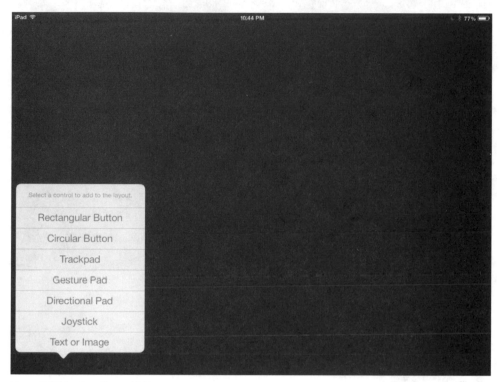

Figure 8.36. Custom Keypad Object menu.

Sibelius Control for iPad by Novatlan Sound
(donations via the programmer's website)
www.novatlan-sound.de/sibeliuscontrol/

Sibelius Control for iPad is a custom keypad layout that was created by Tobias Escher using the Custom Keyboard app mentioned above. This is not an app download from the App Store. Rather, it is a file that is downloaded from the developer's website to your computer and then e-mailed to your iPad as an attachment. The current version only works with Mac computers.

Custom Keypad connects with your computer via VNC, so there is no special application required; just activate screen sharing. It enables the remote control of Sibelius Music Notation software directly from your iPad. The buttons trigger the keystroke commands in Sibelius, allowing you to bypass the computer's keyboard. Available commands include assistance with note entry, editing, adding elements to the score, changing score views, printing, and saving.

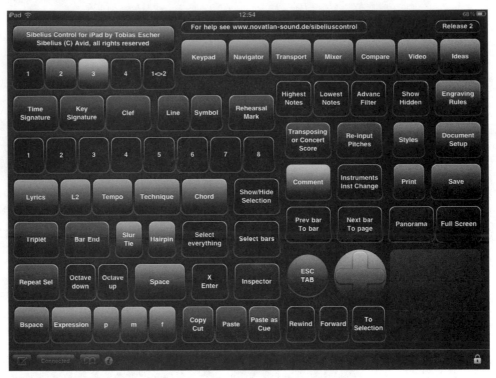

Figure 8.37. Sibelius Control.

VIDEO 8.19. SIBELIUS CONTROL FOR IPAD.

Figure 8.38
http://youtu.be/_P8IMZyvmUo

NumPad—Wireless Numeric Keypad by BitBQ LLC ($4.99)
https://itunes.apple.com/us/app/numpad-wireless-numeric-keypad/id297623436?mt=8

NumPad is an app that turns your iPad or iPhone into a numeric keypad that wirelessly connects with Mac or PC. If you use a Mac with OS X 10.4 or later, NumPad does not require any additional software on your computer. It connects through screen sharing. Windows users will need VNC server software (like RealVNC). This is especially helpful for laptop users who would ordinarily need to purchase a separate USB numeric keypad. NumPad has special layouts for both Finale and Sibelius music notation software main keypads, which display the rhythms, characters, and functions that are assigned to each key.

Figure 8.39. Finale keypad.

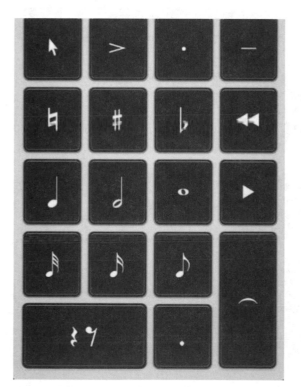

Figure 8.40. Sibelius keypad.

Audio Interfaces for Recording

Audio interfaces lack front panel controls because they are designed to be paired with computer software that manages their operation. The iPad can fill the role of computer and wirelessly connect with the interface, giving the engineer full control while allowing the interface box to be mounted in a remote equipment rack.

PreSonus AB1818VSL Remote by PreSonus Audio Electronics (free)
https://itunes.apple.com/us/app/presonus-ab1818vsl-remote/id531541393?mt=8

The AB1818-VSL iPad app controls the 1818VSL USB audio interface (see chapter 6) remotely over a wireless network when the 1818VSL USB audio interface is used with a Mac or PC computer. The technology and software is borrowed from PreSonus's AI Series mixers that will be mentioned later in this chapter.

The Overview page displays levels, mute, panning, bus assignments, EQ, and compression settings for all channels. For a detailed view of a specific channel's settings, tap the channel number and turn the iPad to portrait orientation, and the display will change to show all data pertaining to that channel. The master channels are displayed in a separate window, accessed by tapping the Masters button at the top of the screen. There are additional views for the Aux Mixer and the app's settings. You can assign names to all the inputs and aux channels for easy identification. With the addition of the app features and the AudioBox 1818VSL hardware, the app becomes an interface and rack mixer combo.

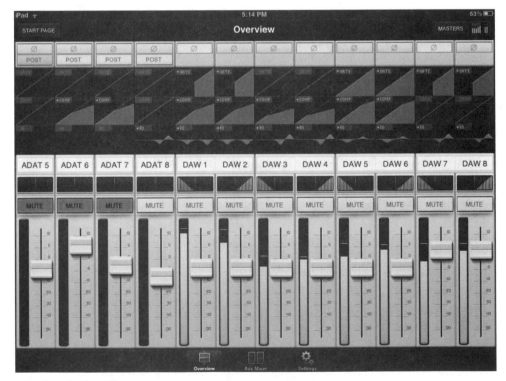

Figure 8.41. AB1818-VSL.

VIDEO 8.20. AB1818-VSL DEMO.

Figure 8.42
http://youtu.be/l29oc4_QDjY

JoeCoRemote by JoeCo (free)
https://itunes.apple.com/us/app/joecoremote/id658901633?mt=8

JoeCoRemote is a free app that controls the JoeCo Blackbox Recorder ($1,995–$4,995) and Blackbox Player. The Blackbox Recorder is a hardware unit designed to record live multitrack audio to a removable USB 2 hard drive. The 96 kHz/24-bit audio files can later be imported into a computer software DAW for mixing or archiving. The Blackbox Recorder is available in several models according to the type of inputs. Models can record from 24 to 64 simultaneous audio tracks based on the type of inputs. Units can be chained to increase the track count.

The JoeCo Blackbox Player ($2,994.50–$4,494.50) is capable of playing up to 64 simultaneous tracks of 96 kHz/ 24-bit audio files from a USB 2 hard drive or flash drive. It is used for in-concert or show playback of prerecorded tracks, complex soundtracks for theme park attractions, or playing back prerecorded tracks for sound checks at show venues.

Both Blackbox units are a single rack space in size (19 x 2 inches) and can be mounted in equipment racks. A wireless router is necessary to create a network connection for the iPad, which functions as a remote control for both devices. A wired connection is also supplied if a Wi-Fi connection is not available. The app provides transport controls, level metering, editing playlists, and triggering playlists during performance.

The Blackbox Recorder allows you to record many tracks without hauling a large Pro Tools or other DAW system when you don't need all the editing and processing capabilities the DAW offers.

Figure 8.43. JoeCoRemote.

VIDEO 8.21. JOECOREMOTE DEMO.

Figure 8.44
http://youtu.be/g6vFiGbQjh8

Network Mixers and Monitors

The mixers in this section are powerful tools for studio and live music production. A complete review of these products is beyond the scope of this book, which only includes each product's iPad and iPhone integration.

With the addition of a wireless router, each mixer frees the engineer from the mixing console, allowing him or her to tweak the mix from anywhere in the venue or studio. All mixers and apps prominently feature live performance applications, but they also have a place in the studio. Individual control over the monitor mix is a feature that is helpful to musicians in a studio. Self-recorders can use their iPad to remotely control a software DAW and either their iPhone or a second iPad to control monitoring while both devices sit side by side on a music stand or in individual stand mounts.

There is a choice between mixers that use the iPad as the primary interface and others that use the iPad as an add-on to traditional mixer hardware. The one drawback to relying too much on an iPad is that you lose the mixer if there is a technical problem with it. Therefore, having a back-up plan such as a second iPad is always a good idea.

Behringer X32 Series Mixers
www.behringer.com/en/Products/X32.aspx
- X32 by Behringer ($2,799.99)
- X32 Compact by Behringer ($1,999,99)
- X32 Producer by Behringer ($1,499.99)
- X32 Rack by Behringer ($1,199.99)
- X32 Core by Behringer ($799.00)

The mixers in the Behringer X32 series use a conventional mixer front panel (except for the rack-mounted models) with iPad control available when a wireless router is connected. The mixer connects to the router using an Ethernet cable. Up to 10 iOS devices can be supported on the network.

The Rack and Core versions of the X32 are frequently used with a laptop computer running the free X32-Edit software, or the iPad running the X32-Mix app. A review of both apps follows in this chapter. An optional expansion card can turn the X32 into an audio interface for Mac or PC computers and other stand-alone recording equipment.

The free iPad app allows the engineer to mix from any position in the concert hall or recording studio. The network also supports iPhones and iPads running the X32 Q app for band member monitor mixes. The X32 has a dedicated resting place for an iPhone on the right side of the mixer. It's the perfect location for running an audio analysis app (see chapter 5) for setting the system up and checking the mix throughout the concert or recording session. The X32 mixer's firmware can be updated via software downloaded to a computer and transferred using USB flash drive.

Figure 8.45. Behringer X32 mixer.

VIDEO 8.22. X32 IPAD SETUP DEMO.

Figure 8.46
http://youtu.be/RisOvJABh4I

X32-Mix by MUSIC Group Research UK Limited (free)
https://itunes.apple.com/us/app/x32-mix/id542646451?mt=8

The X32-Mix app is free. When it is connected to the X32 via a wireless network, you can control all 32 mic inputs, 8 Aux inputs, and 16 buses, plus the effects returns and the main and monitor out levels. The app can also control 16 different monitor mixes, which the engineer can check and adjust from the stage.

The home page of the app is the full mixer view where you can see all channels. There is a Detail page where a single channel's settings, including effects and routing, can be viewed and edited. The Scenes page allows the creation and naming of scenes for instant mixer changes. The Meters page allows all routings to be displayed as meters, but the meter strip at the top of the screen is viewable in all pages of the app. The Recorder page controls the stereo recorder software that is built into the mixer for archival recordings. The Routing page shows all signal chain routings available in the mixer. The final page is the Monitor page. It controls levels and talkback, and there is an oscillator section for generating test tones.

Figure 8.47. X32-Mix Mixer page.

VIDEO 8.23. X32-MIX DEMO.

Figure 8.48.
http://youtu.be/8NkmSW_gZ6Q

X32-Q by MUSIC Group Research UK Limited (free)
https://itunes.apple.com/us/app/x32-q/id587363794?mt=8

X32-Q is a free app that conncets iPhones and iPads to a Wi-Fi network to control monitor mixes from the X32 mixer. The app is compatible with the iPhone, iPad Mini, and iPad. The X32-Q can be used with wedge or in-ear monitor systems.

The app displays a view of the full mixer when in landscape orientation. Switch to portrait orientation, and the view changes to four banks. Each bank can be assigned to a specific mixer channel or subgroup in the mixer. The user has a choice between a fader or a wheel for adjusting the volume levels. Return to landscape orientation to adjust levels of individual channels and further refine the mix.

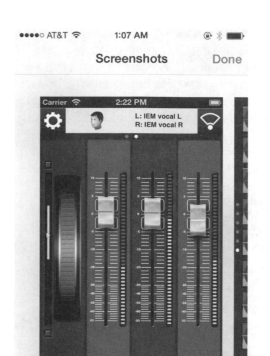

Figure 8.49. X32-Q.

VIDEO 8.24. X32-Q DEMO.

Figure 8.50
http://youtu.be/bOjHV37YBBA

Mackie DL Series Mixers

www.mackie.com/products/dlseries/

- DL806 8 Channel Mixer by Mackie ($799.99) (iPad not included)
- DL1608 16 Channel Mixer by Mackie ($999.99) (iPad not included)

The Mackie DL mixer series uses the iPad both as the software brain of the mixer and its user interface. On the front panel of the mixer is a dock, enabling the iPad to be fastened for security or removed for remote mixing via Wi-Fi. There are 30-pin and Lightning versions of each model. The Lightning version can be used with the iPad Mini. Mackie makes an adapter tray to hold the Mini securely in the proper position to dock with the mixer base. Both the DL806 and the DL1608 use the same app, Master Fader, for all mixer operations; a review of the app follows.

With the addition of a wireless router, the iPad can be removed from the mixer doc for mobile use, allowing the engineer to move around the concert venue and listen to the mix from any perspective to ensure the best possible sound. All of the mixer's functions and features are available while the iPad is operating wirelessly. Up to 10 iOS devices can be connected to the network at once, so the performers can connect to the network using Mackie's My Fader app, which will be mentioned later in this chapter. Now the performers are in control of their own monitor mixes by using a separate iPad or iPhone.

Figure 8.51. Mackie DL1608.

VIDEO 8.25. DL1608 DEMO.

Figure 8.52.
http://youtu.be/_in07Dj8pkM

Mackie Master Fader by Mackie (free)

https://itunes.apple.com/us/app/mackie-master-fader/id511500747?mt=8

The Master Fader Control is a DAW-like app that controls all functions of the DL series mixers. Its mixer and effects sections look similar to a Logic or Pro Tools type of interface. There are two views: a Mixer view, where all channels are visible, and a Channel view, where the EQ settings for each channel are chosen. When you touch a controller on the iPad's screen, Mackie's Grow and Glow feature provides visual feedback by enlarging the controller you've touched and placing a colored halo around it. Horizontal swiping handles navigation up and down the 16 mixer channels. You can create channel groups, so only specific channels are visible at one time. Two adjacent tracks are combined into one stereo track with a single fader to control the left and right channels. Icons or photos can be used for the virtual scribble strip at the bottom of the screen to easily identify which instrument is on a specific track.

On the right side of the screen, next to the Main output fader, is a selection strip for the six aux channels, reverb, and delay. Tap a destination in the strip, and the display changes to show the levels for each channel going to an aux channel or effect. The Master Fader app is able to save scenes and shows so you can recall them as needed. In Master Fader, you can limit the level of control that devices running My Fader have over the monitor mixes. Each device can be set up according to the performer's personal preferences.

One feature of a software-based product such as an iPad app is that it can be updated. When new features are added, an upgrade provides owners with the latest version of the product, and updates are usually free.

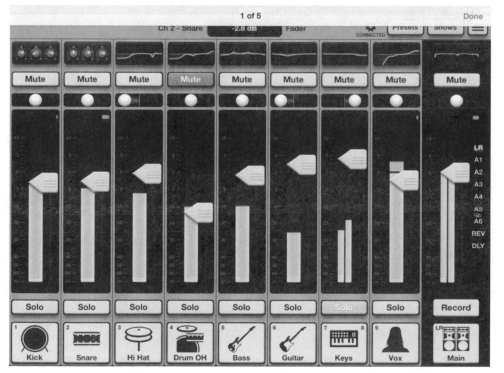

Figure 8.53. Master Fader control.

VIDEO 8.26. MASTER FADER CONTROL DEMO.

Figure 8.54
http://youtu.be/xc981E6Mdhw

Mackie My Fader by Mackie (free)

https://itunes.apple.com/us/app/mackie-my-fader/id599029732?mt=8

My Fader is an app for use on a wireless network with the Mackie DL Series mixers. All performers can download the free app and run it on an iPhone or iPad. Its appearance is similar to the Master Fader app but with limited controls.

With it you can monitor the main outputs or any of the six aux outputs, depending on the engineer's preferences. Musicians can tweak their own mixes from the stage.

My Fader has the same Glow and Grow feature as Master Fader, so controls on the screen enlarge and are outlined by a halo while being adjusted. You can use snapshots for instant changes during a show.

My Fader can be used with wedge and in-ear monitor systems. It requires iOS 6 or later, iPhone 4 or later, and the fourth-generation iPod touch or later. The Master Fader app is also required to be present on the network for mixer functionality.

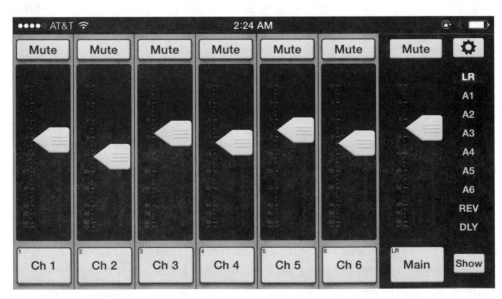

Figure 8.55. My Fader.

VIDEO 8.27. MY FADER.

Figure 8.56
http://youtu.be/w_SfqmAuQWY

V2Mix™ by Pivitec, LLC (free)

https://itunes.apple.com/us/app/v2mix-pro/id626286185?mt=8

This V2Mix app is part of a monitor system that is intended for use in live performance as an add-on to a house or band sound system. V2Mix is free, and it wirelessly controls the Pivitec Personal Monitoring System. The system consists of a hardware input module ($967), which is fed audio from the mixing console. The input module feeds audio to an Ethernet switch ($665) via an Ethernet cable. A wireless router is connected to the switch to create the network for the iPads. A wired Ethernet connection is fed from the switch to a small box, mountable on a mic stand or music stand, containing a 32-channel mixer ($633 each) and a 1/4-inch headphone connector. The mixer has a 1/8-inch line in that is local, so a drummer can connect a metronome to use as a click, and it will not be heard across the system.

Once the app is paired with the network in its settings, you can enter names for all of the channels on the network. Musicians can control the levels and panning in their monitors. Channels can be linked into groups, so, for example, all drum tracks can be linked together for faster adjustment of all drum levels. You can save presets for instant changes during a performance. There is a three-band EQ and a limiter that is applied to all tracks.

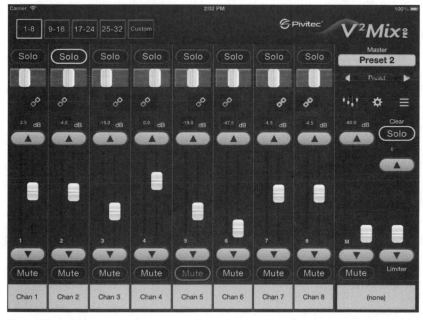

Figure 8.57. V2Mix.

VIDEO 8.28. V2MIX DEMO.

Figure 8.58
http://youtu.be/Y4AR6KzVzNo

PreSonus StudioLive AI-Series Mixers
http://presonus.com/products/StudioLive-AI-Series

- StudioLive 16.4.2AI by PreSonus ($1,999.95)
- StudioLive 24.4.2AI by PreSonus ($2,999.95)
- StudioLive 32.4.2 AI by PreSonus ($3,999.95)

The PreSonus AI (Active Integration) series of mixers consists of conventional hardware mixers with faders, buttons, and rotary control knobs. The network connectivity available is not conventional. A wireless router can be connected to the mixer either through a USB connection or a standard Ethernet connection. This enables an iPad running the SL Remote-AI app (mentioned later in this chapter) to wirelessly control all key mixer functions from anywhere in the performance venue. Musicians can control their own monitor mixes from the stage using the QMix-AI app (mentioned later in this chapter) on their iPhone or iPad. All three models of the AI-Series function identically when it comes to wireless networking and iOS device integration.

> **Tip:** For easy setup, AI-Series mixer users can name their wireless network "StudioLive," with the password "studiolive," and the mixer will automatically connect to it with no additional configuration required.

Figure 8.59. StudioLive 16.4.2AI.

VIDEO 8.29. STUDIOLIVE 16.4.2AI DEMO.

Figure 8.60
http://youtu.be/MOCaVOrhFVE

PreSonus SL Remote-AI by PreSonus Audio Electronics (free)

https://itunes.apple.com/us/app/presonus-sl-remote-ai/id703205978?mt=8

SL Remote-AI is a free iPad app for remotely controlling the AI-Series mixer over a wireless network. Once the mixer is connected to a wireless router and the network is established in the mixer's software, the iPad can join the network when you select it in the settings and enter the password.

The Overview page displays the levels, mutes, panning, bus assignments, EQ, and compression settings for all channels. For a detailed view of a specific channel's settings, tap the channel number and turn the iPad to portrait orientation, and the display will change to show all data pertaining to that channel. The master channels are displayed in a separate window, accessed by tapping the Masters button at the top of the screen. There are additional views for the Aux Mixer, Graphic EQ, and Scenes settings. There is a Talk button that you can use remotely, via the iPad's internal mic. In the setting window, you can assign the talkback to the Main output, one of the three pairs of aux channels, or any combination of those four routings. It is also possible to assign names to all the channels, aux channels, and subgroup channels for easy identification.

Figure 8.61. SL Remote-AI.

VIDEO 8.30. SL REMOTE-AI DEMO.

Figure 8.62
http://youtu.be/vPZTm5AF6fE

PreSonus QMix-AI by PreSonus Audio Electronics (free)
https://itunes.apple.com/us/app/presonus-qmix-ai/id703208043?mt=8

QMix-AI is a free iPhone, iPad touch, or iPad app for controlling personal monitor mixes on the AI-Series mixers. An iOS device can join the network when you select it in the settings and enter the password. There is a Lockout mode in the mixer's software, so you can password protect the mixer's settings to keep intruders from commandeering the mixer, even if they have the network password.

Musicians can have full control of an aux mix to create their own monitor mix. It is possible to limit control for musicians who do not want to create a full mix for themselves. This can be as simple as two parameters: the musician's mix and a mix for everyone else in the band. The level is controlled by the "Wheel of Me," a virtual wheel on the iOS device screen that raises or lowers the controlling musician's level in relation to the rest of the band.

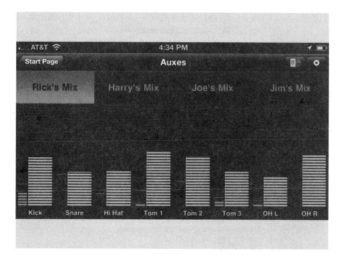

Figure 8.63. QMix-AI.

VIDEO 8.31. QMIX-AI DEMO.

Figure 8.64
http://youtu.be/12O5R0uK1HQ

Roland M Series Mixers

M-480 48 Channel Mixer by Roland Systems Group ($7,995.00)
www.roland.com/products/en/M-480/

M-300 32 Channel Mixer Roland Systems Group ($3,995.00)
www.roland.com/products/en/M-300/

M-200i 32 Channel Mixer Roland Systems Group ($2,995.00)
www.roland.com/products/en/M-200i/

The Roland M-480, M-300, and M200i mixers have the capability to be remotely controlled from the iPad. The mixers require the Roland WNA1100-RL Wireless USB Adapter ($52.99 list price) and a wireless router to establish the network. If a router is not available, you can establish an ad-hoc network using just the Wireless USB Adapter. An ad-hoc network does not rely on existing infrastructure such a wireless router. Once the network is established, up to three iPads can simultaneously control the mixers.

As of this writing, Roland has no separate monitor app for individual musicians. Instead they suggest using the M-48 Personal Mixer ($995) for controlling monitor mixes onstage. There is also a potential "traffic jam" when it comes to the mixer's USB port. The wireless network requires the USB Adapter to be present, but the mixer's recording function uses a flash drive connected to the same port for its audio files. You can't record using the mixer's record feature and have the wireless network running at the same time.

The iPad works as a remote controller for the mixer, allowing the engineer to adjust mixer levels, effects settings and levels, panning, solo tracks, and mute tracks from anywhere in the concert venue. When used next to the mixer, the iPad can function as a second screen display for the M-300 and M-480.

The M-200i is the smallest of the three mixers and uses the iPad as both a remote controller and, using a wired connection to the 30-pin or Lightning port, its visual interface. The mixer has an iPad stand built in for holding it in place while connected.

Figure 8.65. Roland M-200i.

VIDEO 8.32. ROLAND M480 IPAD CONTROL DEMO.

Figure 8.66.
http://youtu.be/kr-wCTDW_40

M-480 Remote by Roland Systems Group (free)
https://itunes.apple.com/us/app/m-480-remote/id555563958?mt=8

M-300 Remote by Roland Corporation (free)
https://itunes.apple.com/us/app/m-300-remote/id621204750?mt=8

M-200i Remote by Roland Corporation (free)
https://itunes.apple.com/us/app/m-200i-remote/id588276040?mt=8

Each of the M-series mixers has its own app, but the look and operation of each app is identical. When you are sitting at the M-480 and M-300 mixers, the iPad can function as an auxiliary screen display and controller.

Across the top of the app's display are mini-meters in groups, showing the levels of all channels, aux channels, buses, and main outputs. You can tap on any of those groups to display the fader strips for the selected group in the main display window. Channel controls include fader levels and sends, pan, mute, solo, EQ settings, and EQ copy and paste. Some controls, such as phantom power, channel naming, and gain reduction on gates and compressors, can be viewed on the iPad but not edited.

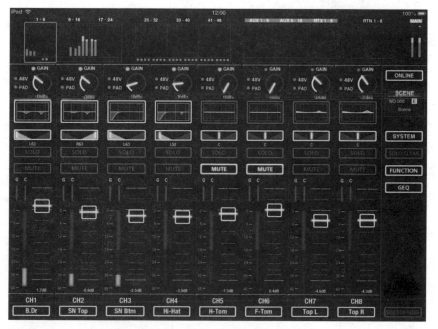

Figure 8.67. M-480 Remote.

VIDEO 8.33. M-480 REMOTE OVERVIEW.

Figure 8.68
http://youtu.be/0vBSqOjn6kU

Studio Options

The studio options presented here use the iPad as a remote control device for either a computer-based DAW program or a hardware mixer. These setups can be used in a live performance situation or as a recording studio set-up.

Ableton Live Control Studio

This configuration combines an iPad and the apps capable of controlling Ableton Live DAW software on a computer. The price does not include the purchase of Ableton Live or the computer.

- iPad 2 or later: starting at $499.00
- Controller or controller programmer apps: $14.99–$49.99

Total cost including iPad: $513.99–$548.99

Multi-app DAW Control

This configuration sets up the iPad to control all your software DAWS, either using prepackaged templates or an app for creating your own.

- iPad 2 or later: starting at $499.00
- Controller or controller programmer apps: $4.99–$49.99

Total cost including iPad: $503.99–$548.99

Eight-Channel Studio

This setup includes both the PreSonus Audiobox 1818VSL and the Mackie DL806 as options. A wireless router is not included.

- iPad 2 or later: starting at $499.00
- eight-channel mixer: $499.95–$799.99

Total cost including iPad: $998.95–$1,298.99

16- to 24-Channel Mixer Studio

The mid-size track count brings some interesting choices between the iPad interface of the Mackie and the traditional PreSonus mixer layout. A wireless router is not included.

- iPad 2 or later: starting at $499.00
- 16- to 24-channel mixer: $999.00–$2,999.95

Total cost including iPad: $1,498.99–$3,498.95

32- to 48-Channel Mixer Studio

To keep the comparison between units with a control surface, this configuration does not include the Behringer Core or Rack mixers, and a wireless router is not included.

- iPad 2 or later: starting at $499.00
- 32- to 48-channel mixer: $1,499.00–$7,995.00

Total cost including iPad: $1,999.99–$8,494.00

Chapter 8 Activities

1. Download the free app Logic Remote, and experiment with GarageBand or Logic if you have one of them installed on a Mac computer.
2. Download any of the free mixer control apps mentioned in this chapter, and evaluate the look and layout. Is layout something that would influence your purchase?
3. From what you learned in activity 2, try designing a basic eight-channel mixer layout in MIDI Designer.
4. Download the free version of MIDI Designer; design a volume controller and make it work with your setup.

Summary

In this chapter, the iPad's versatility in both the studio and live performance was illustrated. The iPad is here to stay, having been embraced by developers of both hardware and software. No matter what tasks you had in mind when you purchased your iPad, it's a good bet you've discovered more possibilities, and there are plenty more to come.

Chapter 9

DISTRIBUTING AND MARKETING YOUR MUSIC

This chapter focuses on marketing and distributing your music and sharing your tracks with others using online file storage. Copyright and licensing will also be introduced.

Uploading and Sharing Files

You will certainly want to share your music with others, perhaps sharing an arrangement with fellow band members for review. Or if you have finished the final mix of your track, you can share it with the world. There are many options to choose from.

Every iPad app has a share option, so you can either e-mail the file to yourself or upload it from a computer. In some cases, you can upload the file to a sharing site directly from the app.

Dropbox by Dropbox (free)
https://itunes.apple.com/us/app/dropbox/id327630330?mt=8

The cloud was introduced in chapter 1, and the idea of using Dropbox for file storage was mentioned, as this is an easy and convenient way to upload and share files of any kind. If you are going to include large audio and/or video files, you will use up the free space quickly, so you may want to remove old files and/or upgrade to a paid account that includes more storage: www.dropbox.com/upgrade.

VIDEO 9.1 SHARING A DROPBOX LINK.

Figure 9.1
http://youtu.be/L67GwOmymwQ

SoundCloud: stream music and listen to playlists by SoundCloud Ltd. (free)
https://itunes.apple.com/us/app/soundcloud/id336353151

SoundCloud has been mentioned throughout this book. It is an excellent place to upload and share your music. The sharing aspect will be featured later in this chapter. There are three types of accounts: Free, Pro, and Pro Unlimited. I suggest starting with the free subscription and then going Pro if you need the storage and additional features.

Many apps—including a number of the apps listed in chapter 7, such as Cubasis and Music Studio—include the option of uploading directly to SoundCloud from within the app. For a list of apps that can directly upload to SoundCloud, go to http://soundcloud.com/apps.

VIDEO 9.2 INTRODUCTION TO USING SOUNDCLOUD.

Figure 9.2
http://youtu.be/ac_O7hF4FCQ

Kompoz by Kompoz (free)
https://itunes.apple.com/us/app/kompoz/id335020996?mt=8

There is a growing list of options for sharing and collaborating with other musicians online. One of the longest-running sites is Kompoz: www.kompoz.com/music/home. Kompoz offers a free account, which you can use to create a profile and submit your own tracks for others to review and collaborate with. There is no storage limit to the files that can be uploaded. There is a music player that features music from Kompoz members, which can be accessed from the website or the iPad app. Kompoz offers paid account options, including more audio formats, the option to do private sessions, and a discount on Abbey Road mastering services.

VIDEO 9.3 INTRODUCTION TO KOMPOZ.

Figure 9.3
http://youtu.be/Wq_OYEf_QnE

Selling Your Music Online

Making money in the music business has changed drastically with the advent of digital streaming and online purchases. Often, bands make most of their money from touring; and record stores, except for used CD stores, have all but disappeared.

It is certainly a challenge to make money selling your music, but there are other benefits to the digital world. By selling your music with a variety of online services, you can make money. There's no guarantee you can make a living by selling your music online, but it can be an income stream at the very least. There are many services for selling music online, both digitally and via traditional CDs.

Direct or Reseller

There are two approaches to take with reselling your digital music tracks. You can go directly to the digital stores, such as iTunes, Amazon, and Google Play, or you can use a company that will distribute your music for you through a host of online sellers. The latter is the easiest option.

Three of the top companies to consider are CD Baby, TuneCore, and ReverbNation. You can read a comparison of these three services at www.recordseattle.com/recordseattle/ReverbNation_vs_Tunecore.html.

1. CD Baby (http://members.cdbaby.com): An online music store specializing in the sale of CDs and music downloads from independent musicians to consumers. The company is also a digital aggregator of independent music recordings, distributing content to several online music retailers.
2. TuneCore (www.tunecore.com): A company similar to CD Baby, offering both digital and CD sales.
3. ReverbNation (www.reverbnation.com): As of this writing, only offers digital sales.

Promotion

In order to get your music out into the masses, you have to do a little bit of work and find places where others can learn about your music. These include hosting your own website and using social media, as well as other cloud services such as SoundCloud and YouTube.

Weebly by Weebly Inc. (free)
https://itunes.apple.com/us/app/weebly/id511158309?mt=8

If you don't already have your own website, you can create one to promote your music to others. There are a plethora of options for creating free websites. The one that I have found to be the simplest is www.weebly.com. You can create and update your own website or blog from your computer or via their iPad app. There is a free version and a paid Pro option that offers more features and services: http://weeblyfeatures.weebly .com/weebly-pro-features.html.

VIDEO 9.4. INTRODUCTION TO WEEBLY.COM.

Figure 9.4
http://youtu.be/aBdOgTj7x7o

SoundCloud

SoundCloud was listed previously in this chapter as an option for storing and sharing your files. It is also an excellent way to promote your music. Think of SoundCloud as part social media and part Dropbox. SoundCloud is a social media site, focusing on audio posts that can be finished tracks or works in progress. Visitors to your SoundCloud page, which could include your students, can listen, comment, and collaborate. It can be an excellent place to showcase audio files or the work of your students.

You can follow other artists in the same manner as "friending" someone on Facebook and get notifications when they post new material, or you can just listen to what others are posting. You can search the membership for specific artists or styles of music, and like or post comments on favorite tracks. You can access your account through a web browser or the SoundCloud app on a mobile device. You can also share files posted on SoundCloud—yours or others—through your accounts with Facebook, Twitter, and Tumblr. Here are some tips to help promote your music on SoundCloud:

1. Send your SoundCloud links to bloggers and people who might promote your music.
2. Be sure you share works that are not completely finished privately. Only share your best tracks publicly.
3. SoundCloud allows you to offer free tracks for download. Consider offering one or more of your tracks as a free download.
4. Follow others on SoundCloud who produce similar music or might be a possible resource for promoting your music.
5. Include "Buy Links" with your SoundCloud tracks that are not offered as free downloads, so people can purchase your tracks using CD Baby, one of the services listed later in this chapter.

VIDEO 9.5 PROMOTING WITH SOUNDCLOUD.

Figure 9.5
http://youtu.be/T_0bf0ymw14

Spotify Music by Spotify Ltd. (free/Premium: $10 per month)
https://itunes.apple.com/us/app/spotify-music/id324684580?mt=8

You can get your music on Spotify to share with the millions of users in a variety of ways. The easiest is to contact one of the companies called aggregators that Spotify has an agreement with. Then, you can share your music on Spotify and receive royalties when the tracks are played. For more information, go to www.spotify.com/us/about-us/labels/.

Music Videos: YouTube

This book is about sound and audio, but you can also use video streaming services such as YouTube to promote your music. Creating a YouTube channel and promoting your music is free. There is a wonderful resource produced by DIY Musician. They offer a complete publication on ways to promote your music on YouTube: http://diymusician.cdbaby.com/musician-guides/the-diy-musicians-complete-guide-to-youtube/.

YouTube by Google Inc. (free)
https://itunes.apple.com/us/app/youtube/id544007664?mt=8

By creating your own YouTube channel, you can include videos of your music and links to purchase them on iTunes, CD Baby, and other services. You can use iMovie on Mac or Movie Maker on Windows to create videos with your audio and then upload them to YouTube.

Social Networking

You will want to use every option for promoting your music, including Twitter, Facebook, and Instagram. Each of these tools offers a host of options.

Twitter by Twitter Inc. (free)
https://itunes.apple.com/us/app/twitter/id333903271?mt=8

Use Twitter to follow similar artists and promote your new tracks and offerings.

Facebook by Facebook Inc. (free)
https://itunes.apple.com/us/app/facebook/id284882215?mt=8

Create a Facebook page specifically designed for your music. Promote live events and other activities to showcase you and your music.

Instagram by Instagram Inc. (free)
https://itunes.apple.com/us/app/instagram/id389801252?mt=8

When you are touring, there is a lot of downtime when you can promote your music on various social media sites, such as Twitter, Facebook, and Instagram. Check out this blog with some helpful and insightful ways to promote your music on Instagram.

Figure 9.6. Mashable Blog: Instagram
http://mashable.com/2011/06/12/instagram
-bands/?utm_source=feedburner&utm
_medium=feed&utm_campaign=Feed%3A+Mashable+
%28Mashable%29#164391-Share-Across-All-Social
-Networks

Below is an interview with composer Brian Lowdermilk on how he uses social media to promote his work.

VIDEO 9.6 INTERVIEW WITH BRIAN LOWDERMILK.

Figure 9.7.
http://vimeo.com/87766948

Copyright and Licensing

It is beyond the scope of this book to include a complete guide to copyright and licensing. Rather, this is intended as an overview to help you with decisions on what you can produce and when you need to get permission to arrange and produce music. An excellent reference on copyright in the print medium is the Music Publishers Association website: www.mpa.org. There is a copyright area of the site that offers an excellent overview, written in layman's terms.

Another excellent resource is on the SoundCloud site: https://soundcloud.com/pages/copyright.

Figure 9.8 SoundCloud copyright center.

What is the Copyright Law?

The rights given to a copyright holder include the exclusive rights to reproduce the copyrighted works; to prepare derivative works based on the copyrighted music; to sell, rent, lend, or transfer ownership of copies; and to perform the copyrighted musical work publicly or by means of an audio transmission. Read more about this on the Music Teachers National Association website: www.mtna.org/member-resources/copyright-information/.

Public Domain

Public Domain refers to music that is no longer covered by the copyright law and is therefore free to the public. You can arrange, reproduce, perform, record, or publish it, and use or sell it commercially as you like. Most musical works published with a valid copyright notice of 1922 or earlier are in the public domain in the United States. So all of these compositions can be arranged by teachers and students without violating the copyright law. You can search for titles in public domain at www.pdinfo.com.

Mechanical Rights

Mechanical licensing is the licensing of copyrighted musical compositions for use on CDs, records, tapes, and certain digital configurations. This includes original arrangements that you have composed of pieces that are currently under copyright and not in public domain. The Harry Fox Agency (www.harryfox.com) was established as an agency to license, collect, and distribute royalties on behalf of musical copyright owners.

If you want to produce fewer than 2,500 copies of your recording as either physical products (CDs, cassettes, and vinyl) or permanent digital downloads, Harry Fox suggests you request your licenses using HFA Songfile: www.harryfox.com/public/songfile.jsp. If you plan on making more than 2,500 copies, open a Harry Fox Agency Licensee Account: www.harryfox.com/public/Licensee.jsp.

> **Tip:** Of course there is an app for that. Check out the Copyright and Mechanical Rights app. It costs $19.99 and includes a host of helpful information on the topic: https://itunes.apple.com/us/app/music-business-101-copyright/id587589436?mt=12.

Performing Rights Organizations, or PROs

Performing rights are the right to perform music in public. This is part of copyright law and demands payment to the music's composer/lyricist and publisher, with the royalties generally split 50/50 between the two. *Public performance* means that a musician or group that is not the copyright holder is performing a piece of music live, as opposed to the playback of a prerecorded song. Performances are considered "public" if they take place in a public place and the audience is outside of a normal circle of friends and family, such as at concerts and nightclubs. Public performance also includes broadcast and cable television, radio, and any other transmitted performance of a live song.

Permission to publicly perform a song must be obtained from the copyright holder or a collective rights organization. When someone pays for the right to perform one of your compositions, the concept is that an organization collects the fees and they are shared with you, the composer.

There are three popular performing rights organizations. Anyone can join BMI (Broadcast Music Company) (www.bmi.com) or ASCAP (American Society of Composers, Authors and Publishers) (www.ascap.com). SESAC (Society of European Stage Authors and Composers) (www.sesac.com) is by invitation only. So the two organizations to consider joining are BMI and ASCAP. They do essentially the same thing, and they will pay you a royalty if there is money to collect for your musical works and you meet their requirements to receive money after you join.

ASCAP Mobile by ASCAP (free)
https://itunes.apple.com/us/app/ascap-mobile/id388644789?mt=8

BMI Mobile by Broadcast Music Inc. (free)
https://itunes.apple.com/us/app/bmi-mobile/id417482125?mt=8

Chapter 9 Activities

1. Share one of your music tracks on Dropbox or SoundCloud. Copy and share the links to your individual tracks and playlists.
2. Collaborate with other musicians via online services such as Kompoz.
3. Review the options for distributing your music online. Of the three mentioned in this chapter (CD Baby, TuneCore, and ReverbNation), which is best for you?
4. Create a marketing and promotion plan, and include some or all of the areas mentioned in this chapter.
5. Review the performing rights organizations BMI and ASCAP, and join the one that best fits your needs.

Summary

This chapter included options for uploading and sharing your digital music with Dropbox and SoundCloud. Kompoz was introduced as one of the ways to collaborate on projects with other musicians online. The various options for selling your music online, in both digital and CD format, were also covered, along with creating your own website or blog using Weebly.com. The chapter concluded with information on the copyright law in general, along with performance and mechanical rights licensing and information.

INDEX

ABOUT THE AUTHORS

Producer and composer Vincent A. Leonard Jr. has had works premiered nationally and internationally. He is published by Arrangers Publishing Company, Educational Programs Publications, and National Music Works. He is coauthor of *Recording in the Digital World, Finale: An Easy Guide to Music Notation*, and *Sibelius: A Comprehensive Guide to Music Notation*. In 1996, he and fellow producer and engineer Jack Klotz Jr. formed Invinceable Entertainment, from which they have released two CDs, *Magic Up Our Sleeve* and *On the Brink of Tomorrow*. Leonard's compositional credits include theme and episode music for the *Captain Courteous* radio series, numerous theater pieces, and industrials. He has provided orchestrations for world-premier productions of *Redwall* for Opera Delaware, as well as *Elliot and the Magic Bed, Isabell and the Pretty Ugly Spell*, and *The Little Princess* for Upper Darby Summer Stage. Also widely known as a copyist and arranger, he has worked on projects with Peter Nero, the Philly Pops Orchestra, Doc Severinsen, the London Symphony Orchestra, Chuck Mangione, and Leslie Burrs, and on musicals by Duke Ellington, Alan Menken, Kurt Weil, and Mitch Leigh. Leonard is a member of NARAS and ASCAP, and he is active as a clinician and beta tester for music software for Macintosh computers.

Thomas Rudolph, Ed.D., is an adjunct instructor for Berklee Online. He also conducts summer workshops in music technology at Villanova University and Central Connecticut State University. Dr. Rudolph is one of the seminal people in music technology. He began his work as a clinician and workshop leader in the field in 1982. In addition to his work in music technology, Dr. Rudolph is a busy trumpet player in the Philadelphia area and performs with the group Gaudeamus. His compositions and arrangements have been published by Neil Kjos and Northeastern Music Publications Inc. Dr. Rudolph has authored and coauthored many books, including: *Finale: An Easy Guide to Music Notation, Sibelius: A Comprehensive Guide to Sibelius Music Notation Software, Teaching Music with Technology*, and *Recording in the Digital World: YouTube in Music Education and Finding Funds for Music Technology*. He was one of four coauthors of the TI:ME publication *Technology Strategies for Music Education*. Dr. Rudolph is coauthor of the Alfred Music Tech Series, which includes *Playing Keyboard, Music Production and MIDI Sequencing*, and *Composing with Notation Software*. He has published many articles on music technology that have appeared in the *Music Educators Journal, The Instrumentalist*, and *Downbeat* magazine.

quick **PRO**
guides *series*

Ableton Grooves
by Josh Bess
Softcover w/DVD-ROM •
978-1-4803-4574-4 • $19.99

Producing Music with Ableton Live
by Jake Perrine
Softcover w/DVD-ROM •
978-1-4584-0036-9 • $16.99

Sound Design, Mixing, and Mastering with Ableton Live
by Jake Perrine
Softcover w/DVD-ROM •
978-1-4584-0037-6 • $16.99

Mastering Auto-Tune
by Max Mobley
Softcover w/ DVD-ROM •
978-1-4768-1417-9 • $16.99

The Power in Cakewalk SONAR
by William Edstrom, Jr.
Softcover w/DVD-ROM •
978-1-4768-0601-3 • $16.99

Mixing and Mastering with Cubase
by Matthew Loel T. Hepworth
Softcover w/DVD-ROM •
978-1-4584-1367-3 • $16.99

The Power in Cubase: Tracking Audio, MIDI, and Virtual Instruments
by Matthew Loel T. Hepworth
Softcover w/DVD-ROM •
978-1-4584-1366-6 • $16.99

Digital Performer for Engineers and Producers
by David E. Roberts
Softcover w/DVD-ROM •
978-1-4584-0224-0 • $16.99

The Power in Digital Performer
by David E. Roberts
Softcover w/DVD-ROM •
978-1-4768-1514-5 • $16.99

Logic Pro for Recording Engineers and Producers
by Dot Bustelo
Softcover w/DVD-ROM •
978-1-4584-1420-5 • $16.99

The Power in Logic Pro: Songwriting, Composing, Remixing, and Making Beats
by Dot Bustelo
Softcover w/DVD-ROM •
978-1-4584-1419-9 • $16.99

Musical iPad
by Thomas Rudolph and Vincent Leonard
Softcover w/DVD-ROM •
978-1-4803-4244-6 • $19.99

Mixing and Mastering with Pro Tools
by Glenn Lorbecki
Softcover w/DVD-ROM •
978-1-4584-0033-8 • $16.99

Tracking Instruments and Vocals with Pro Tools
by Glenn Lorbecki
Softcover w/DVD-ROM •
978-1-4584-0034-5 •$16.99

The Power in Reason
by Andrew Eisele
Softcover w/DVD-ROM •
978-1-4584-0228-8 • $16.99

Sound Design and Mixing in Reason
by Andrew Eisele
Softcover w/DVD-ROM •
978-1-4584-0229-5 • $16.99

Studio One for Engineers and Producers
by William Edstrom, Jr.
Softcover w/DVD-ROM •
978-1-4768-0602-0 • $16.99

HAL•LEONARD®
quickproguides.halleonardbooks.com
Prices, contents, and availability subject to change without notice.

0813